THE MEDITERRANEAN SEA RULES

THE MEDITERRANEAN SEA RULES

10 God-Given Strategies for Navigating Life's Tempestuous Sea

Robert J. Morgan

The Mediterranean Sea Rules

Cover Design by Brandon Riesgo
Published by Cover to Cover LLC

Hardcover ISBN: 978-0-9884966-7-5
First Edition
Printed in the United States.

To Katrina

Contents

By the Same Author

The Red Sea Rules

The Jordan River Rules

And Other Titles, Including

The 50 Final Events in World History

100 Bible Verses That Made America

Then Sings My Soul: Books 1, 2, and 3

100 Bible Verses Everyone Should Know by Heart

God Works All Things Together for Your Good

The Strength You Need

PREFACE

God moves in a mysterious way, His wonders to perform.
He plants His footsteps in the sea, and rides upon the storm.

—WILLIAM COWPER

Luke the evangelist lay on his stomach, arms wrapped around a supporting post in the sodden cabin. He was drenched to the skin, shivering. His clothes were soaked and salty, and his stomach heaved in agony. As the sea convulsed and the ship lurched in the gale, he could hear timbers cracking. The hull was breaking apart in the storm.

A smaller fellow was sitting beside Luke, clutching a post. One wrist bore a chain, but nothing was attached to the other end. He was free to move about, but movement was nearly impossible on the careening vessel. So he sat, knees to chest, his body trembling from the raw weather. Unlike all the others, however, this man was unafraid. In this storm, at least, he knew he was unsinkable.

This man was the apostle Paul.

The book of Acts concludes with the story of Paul aboard

a doomed ship in a hurricane. The voyage and shipwreck of Paul, as told by Luke, are fascinating but often overlooked. When I originally preached from Acts 27 and 28, I titled the series "Keeping Your Head Above the Water While Your Ship Is Going Down." A couple of years ago, I taught the material again, and my title was "Navigating Life's Tempestuous Sea." This book is the third iteration of the material, and I believe it's a fitting addition to my previously published books *The Red Sea Rules* and *The Jordan River Rules.*

So, friends, welcome aboard *The Mediterranean Sea Rules.*

The Bible is both a storybook and a stormy book. Weather patterns blow through the pages of Scripture like a forecaster's map, from Noah's flood to Jonah's typhoon to the storm-tossed Sea of Galilee. The Lord sent an electrical storm across Egypt that shocked the ancient world (see Exodus 9:24). He spoke to Job out of the whirlwind (see Job 38:1). And Jesus spoke to His disciples on the tempestuous waters of Lake Galilee.

Psalm 135:7 says, "He makes clouds rise from the ends of the earth; He sends lightning with the rain and brings out the wind from His storehouse."

Biblical storms were classrooms where the Divine Prognosticator taught unforgettable lessons, and still does. Nature's weather patterns parallel the conditions of life. How often the storms point to spiritual truths, enabling us to navigate our days!

Atmospheric disturbances come to us all. But the Lord pilots His people over rough waters, imparting the nautical skills necessary for spiritual buoyancy. Paul didn't have time to figure things out during the terrors of his voyage. He was already prepared for adverse winds. His lifelong commitment to spiritual maturity allowed him to survive and to save those with him.

From Acts 27 and 28, I want to draw ten lessons for navigating stormy weather. The same God who rules the tempest will still the storms in your life. His grace will overcome the gale. The Savior who stills the tempest can settle your nerves, direct your voyage, and strengthen your soul.

Let's begin with a hymn of prayer. When I was in graduate school, I learned this classic gospel song that's been a favorite of mine ever since:

Jesus, Savior, pilot me
Over life's tempestuous sea;
Unknown waves before me roll,
Hiding rock and treacherous shoal.
Chart and compass come from Thee.
Jesus, Savior, pilot me.

—EDWARD HOPPER (1871)

PAUL'S JOURNEY TO ROME

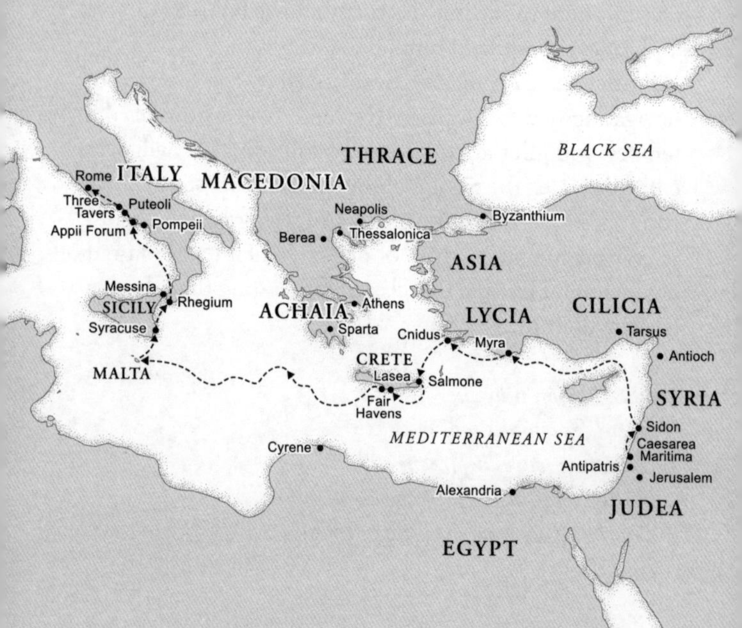

Mediterranean Sea Rule # 1

When Your Plans Collapse, Make Sure You Don't

When it was decided that we would sail for Italy, Paul and some other prisoners were handed over to a centurion named Julius, who belonged to the Imperial Regiment. We boarded a ship from Adramyttium about to sail for ports along the coast of the province of Asia, and we put out to sea. Aristarchus, a Macedonian from Thessalonica, was with us.

—Acts 27:1-2

The Best-Laid Plans

God so attends to the regulations of individual events, and they all so proceed from His set plan, that nothing takes place by chance.

—John Calvin

How could Paul have gotten it so wrong? As he finished his third missionary tour in Acts 20, he paused for three months in Corinth to pray, plan, discuss, strategize, and announce his fourth great campaign (see Acts 20:3). He stayed in a villa belonging to Gaius (see Romans 16:23). His closest associates joined the planning sessions—Timothy, Lucius, Jason, Sosipater, and Tertius (see Romans 16:21).

Paul had collected a large offering from churches in Europe for the impoverished believers in Judea, and he wanted to deliver it in person. From Jerusalem, he intended to head to Rome—a city he had never seen—encouraging the church there and using it as a launching pad to take the gospel to Spain. Some scholars suggest Paul believed he could single-handedly fulfill the Great Commission by getting the message of Jesus to the farthest realms of the then-known world.[1]

From the home of Gaius, Paul wrote to the Romans:

> But now that there is no more place for me to work in these regions, and since I have been longing for many years to visit you, I plan to do so when I go to Spain. I hope to see you while passing through and to have you assist me on my journey there, after I have enjoyed your company for a little while. Now, however, I am on my way to Jerusalem in the service of the Lord's people there. . . .
>
> So after I have completed this task and have made sure that they received this contribution, I will go to Spain and visit you on the way. I know that when I come to you, I will come in the full measure of the blessing of Christ. (Romans 15:23-29)

Having made his plans, Paul committed them to God and sent his letter to Rome by the hand of a remarkable woman named Phoebe (see Romans 16:1), while he and his companions left Corinth for Jerusalem, and then, presumably, on to Rome and Spain and points beyond.

Paul was in Jerusalem barely a week before his plans

fell apart like a child's tower of blocks (see Acts 21:27). His presence provoked a riot and he was nearly killed in the mayhem (see 21:30-31). Roman soldiers seized him, stripped him, and hung him by the wrists. Out came the deadly Roman whips, ready to shred his flesh (see 22:25).

Paul talked his way out of the flogging, but he wouldn't be a free man again for the duration of the book of Acts. When assassins tried to kill him in Jerusalem, he was shipped to the Roman headquarters in Caesarea (see 23:23), where he spent over two years in prison (see 24:27).

He finally appealed his case to the imperial court in Rome, and Acts 27:1 says, "When it was decided that we would sail for Italy . . ."

Notice the grammar: not when Paul decided, or when Luke decided.

Paul was now in the hands of the world's most brutal government, and circumstances were no longer under his control. Though he would eventually make it to Rome, it wasn't as he'd planned. He arrived in chains, and the route there was dangerous and miserable . . .

. . . and planned by Jesus Christ, who had never lost control of a single detail of the unfolding events. As ominous clouds literally rolled over Paul's life, the Lord was carefully navigating his route. Proverbs 16:9 (CSB) says, "A person's heart plans his way, but the Lord determines his steps."

Dr. F. B. Meyer said, "The black clouds are only His

water cisterns, and on the other side they are bathed in sunshine. Do not look at your sorrows in the lowlands of your pilgrimage, but from the uplands of God's purpose."

I take two lessons from this. First, planning is essential. God made us to dream, to envision, and to set our purposes and goals for a strong tomorrow, which Paul did. Second, when our plans are then committed to Him, He navigates the route—and it may be different than we expect.

When, therefore, we commit our plans to Him and they go to pieces, we must not!

One of my dearest friends planned to retire so that he and his wife could take an around-the-world cruise, but the Lord took her to heaven in a car accident. Another friend thought he had met the woman who would become his wife, but she changed her mind and moved away. I planned to be part of the same church for the rest of my life, but things changed and it was a hard loss. Yet the Lord oversees our lives, even over rough seas. He overrules and He overcomes.

We must come to see disappointment as God's way of diverting us from lesser plans to better paths, which unfold with time.

The Lord is orchestrating events you cannot control. He has total foreknowledge of our fortunes and full authority over our misfortunes. We have to trust Him with disruptions, diversions, and detours. When we've committed our lives to Him in utter surrender, we let Him turn breakdowns into breakthroughs and setbacks into springboards.

That's why when Paul's plans fell apart, he didn't.

Neither should you.

Missing the Boat

Jesus replied, "You do not realize now what I am doing, but later you will understand."

—John 13:7

Without the destruction of two great ships, I wouldn't be writing this book.

The first, of course, was Paul's shipwreck in Acts 28, without which this little volume could never have been conceived.

The other was a British transoceanic passenger and cargo steamship named *S.S. City of Lahore*. It had seventy rooms for first-class passengers and forty second-class rooms.[2] This ship sailed into New York Harbor in the fall of 1918 and docked at a pier on the Hudson River, where a man named Robert C. McQuilkin booked a stateroom for his family. With the war ending, Robert and Marguerite McQuilkin were heading overseas for missionary service.

At age seventeen, McQuilkin had given a talk about "the greatest enterprise ever before the world . . . and the only enterprise of any consequence"—global missions.[3] He was personally yielded to God's missionary call and eager to serve the Lord in the "regions beyond."

The McQuilkins counted the cost, applied to the Africa Inland Mission, raised their support, and in due time secured their room on the *City of Lahore*. With them were their three small children. All their equipment and supplies were boarded onto the ship.

While the McQuilkins were offering heartfelt goodbyes to friends in Philadelphia, the *City of Lahore* burst into flame in New York Harbor. Bob was on a Philadelphia streetcar when he saw the headlines. Firefighters pumped the ship full of water and sank it to prevent the flames from spreading up and down the docks.

In those days, few ships ferried passengers around the world. For nearly two years, the McQuilkins waited for another vessel, but their plans were waylaid again and again. Finally in July 1919, Bob wrote to his supporters saying:

> We are writing to let you know the present state of our missionary plans. These plans have suffered many interruptions and changes, which must have tried the patience of our friends and caused them to wonder if we had missed the sure guidance of the Lord. But through it all He had one perfect plan that has not suffered any changes and we can see how every step has

helped toward that plan and every apparent disappointment has served a purpose.[4]

Notice that powerful last phrase: "Every *apparent* disappointment has served a purpose."

Disappointments are God's way of weaving our circumstances into more beautiful patterns than we could have contemplated. Like an artist with multicolored wire, the Lord bends, shapes, coils, braids, plies, pulls, and spins every detail into the handicraft of heaven. Broken dreams become divine schemes in the hands of the Almighty.

The sinking of the *S.S. City of Lahore*, which happened thirty-four years before my birth, changed my life. While waiting for God's open door, Robert C. McQuilkin continued his itinerant ministry preaching the truths of the victorious Christian life. His travels brought him to Columbia, South Carolina, where a group of praying women longed to open a Bible school to train Christian workers.

Dr. McQuilkin became the first president of Columbia International University and infused it with his message of victorious faith. And there in 1971, I yielded my life to vocational Christian service, grew in Christ, was mentored as a Bible teacher, met my wife, Katrina, and launched into the ministry God had for me. Dr. McQuilkin's son, Robertson, was by that time the school's president, and I count him among my mentors.

Dr. and Mrs. McQuilkin never made it into vocational

overseas missionary service, but CIU is one of the world's leading training institutions for global evangelization, with thousands of graduates serving overseas.

The Puritan Thomas Goodwin said in his commentary on Ephesians, "[God] plots everything beforehand. . . . Nothing falls out but what He had laid the plot before."[5]

On the final night of His natural life, Jesus knew His disciples didn't understand what was happening. Events were crashing around them like tumbling boulders, and they didn't know how to manage His imminent arrest and crucifixion. He said, "You do not realize now what I am doing, but later you will understand."

And, later, did they ever!

Take every apparent disappointment as an appointment of God's providence, and recognize that sunken ships don't mean submerged hopes. When your plans fall apart, make sure you don't—for the Lord never will.

He will grant your desires by what He ordains.

HAVE YOU NOT SEEN?

Praise ye the Lord, the Almighty, the King of Creation!
O my soul, praise Him, for He is thy health and salvation.

—JOACHIM NEANDER

All three daughters were with me as we hovered around my wife, Katrina, at Vanderbilt Medical Center and waited for her final breath. The attending doctor prayed with us, and our hearts were breaking. Suddenly Katrina opened her eyes and smiled—and the Lord gave us another blessed month with her. It's perhaps the greatest gift the Lord ever gave me.

The day after Katrina came home from the hospital, we entertained a group of German worship leaders whose visit had been planned for a year. My friend Johannes Schroeder led the group. We catered supper by the pool, and then the group came inside to discuss hymns and worship.

I told them Katrina and I had a favorite German hymn—"Praise Ye the Lord, the Almighty" by Joachim Neander. They sang it as if giving Katrina a private concert, and the videotape of her smiling with every note is one of my greatest possessions. It's as though the Lord sent a special choir from around the world to sing to Katrina as her home-going approached.

The second stanza of Neander's hymn is a powerful affirmation of the overruling providence of God. Apart from the Bible, I know of no better words to encourage us to remember we have a God who misses no details, breaks no promises, and makes no mistakes.

Why not learn this song and sing it before your ship runs into headwinds?

Praise ye the Lord,
Who o'er all things so wondrously reigneth,
Shelters thee under His wings,
yea, so gently sustaineth!
Hast thou not seen how thy desires e'er have been
Granted in what He ordaineth?

Study Questions

1. Read Acts 27:1-2. What happened to Paul that countered his plans to travel to Rome and Spain to preach the gospel? What does that tell us about the way disruptions can seem to hamper our progress for the Lord?

2. Acts 27:1 says, "When it was decided . . ." What does this say about Paul's role in these plans? When is a time you felt like your plans were decided for you, and how did that contradict the plans you had made?

3. Read Proverbs 16:9. How does this verse come to bear on the account of Paul's travel plans before his arrests? What encouragement can we take away from this?

4. Read John 13:7. What confidence can be taken from Jesus' words in this passage?

For further individual or group study, check out *The Mediterranean Sea Rules Study Guide* and *The Mediterranean Sea Rules Video Series,* both available at medsearules.com.

Mediterranean Sea Rule #2

Trust the Slow Work of God

The next day we landed at Sidon; and Julius, in kindness to Paul, allowed him to go to his friends so they might provide for his needs. From there we put out to sea again and passed to the lee of Cyprus because the winds were against us. When we had sailed across the open sea off the coast of Cilicia and Pamphylia, we landed at Myra in Lycia. There the centurion found an Alexandrian ship sailing for Italy and put us on board. We made slow headway for many days and had difficulty arriving off Cnidus. When the wind did not allow us to hold our course, we sailed to the lee of Crete, opposite

Salmone. We moved along the coast with difficulty and came to a place called Fair Havens, near the town of Lasea.

—Acts 27:3-8

God's Infallible Timing

Above all, trust the slow work of God.

—Teilhard de Chardin

I've been intrigued with a young backpacker in Australia named Reuben Schoots. During an eight-month trek through Latin America, he contracted a series of tropical viruses and became bedridden. His constant pain led to an opiate addiction, which cost him his job and his education. As a result, he sank into depression.

One day a friend visited him wearing a beautiful wristwatch with a glass that showed the internal movements. Schoots was fascinated by the synchronicity of the moving parts. He took up the skill of watchmaking and has become a master at the craft, though the work is tiny, exacting, and precise.

Schoots is becoming a famous craftsman and his watches are almost beyond value. One journalist summed it up like this: "While Schoots often has to rest, he appreciates the steady course this new version of his life is taking because, with patience and perseverance, he's got every reason to believe time will be on his side."[6]

When we're in Christ, time is on our side. Even when we suffer delays, setbacks, and interruptions, with patience and perseverance we come to realize His timing is infallible. The Lord manages our lives with the precision of a watchmaker, and His children are never racing against time or running out of time. We're awaiting God's timing and traveling at His speed.

Paul, a man of action, surely reminded himself of that when his voyage stalled.

Nothing in Paul's life astounds me more than how his well-planned strategy for traveling from Jerusalem to Rome to Spain collapsed like a tower of cards. Instead of an exciting fourth missionary tour, he faced a potential Roman flogging, an assassination plot in Jerusalem, two years' incarceration in Caesarea, and nothing but delays and difficulties on this voyage with more to come, followed by another two years' imprisonment.

Yet he accepted what he couldn't change and recalibrated his attitude according to God's schedule. He was ready to go but willing to wait and to redeem the time. His mindset: "Moment by moment, O Lord, I am Thine."

The voyage in Acts 27 took place in the late fall after the Day of Atonement (see verse 9). Here's how Luke described the trip. Notice the eight phrases I've bolded.

We . . . passed to the lee of Cyprus because **the winds**

were against us. When we had sailed across the open sea off the coast of Cilicia and Pamphylia, we landed at Myra in Lycia. There the centurion found an Alexandrian ship sailing for Italy and he put us on board. We made **slow headway for many days** and **had difficulty** arriving off the Cnidus. When the **wind did not allow us** to hold our course, we sailed to the lee of Crete, opposite Salmone. We moved along the coast **with difficulty** and came to a place called Fair Havens, near the town of Lasea. **Much time had been lost**, and sailing had already become **dangerous** because by now it was after the Day of Atonement.

The Roman navy had warships, but most of the vessels plying the Mediterranean were cargo ships. Many of them were vessels ferrying grain from Egypt to the Roman world. They weren't made for passengers, but those willing to pay a fare could travel along, as Paul had done many times in his career. On three prior occasions, he'd been shipwrecked, once stranded at sea overnight, either in a lifeboat or clinging to wreckage (see 2 Corinthians 11:25). He was an experienced mariner, and he sensed the approach of the stormy season.

But there he was nonetheless—not in Rome encouraging the church nor in Spain evangelizing the lost. He was stranded on a merchant ship floating into fatal waters. Yet the Lord was controlling every gust of wind, every swelling wave, the darkening clouds, and the piercing lightning.

The Bible says, "The Lord does whatever pleases Him, in the heavens and on the earth, in the seas and all their depths. He makes clouds rise from the ends of the earth; He sends lightning with the rain and brings out the wind from His storehouse" (Psalm 135:6-7).

Ray Stedman wrote:

> Why would the apostle experience such grave difficulty from natural forces when he is obviously in the center of the will of God, on the way to Rome where the Lord wants him to be? The Lord Jesus had appeared to Paul in Jerusalem and had told him that He wanted him to go to Rome, that He would take him there, and that he must appear before the emperor. And Paul is not disobedient; he is moving right in accord with God's purpose. Nevertheless the winds are contrary and everything else seems to go wrong on this voyage. God, who controls the winds and the waves, could surely have made it easy for Paul to get to Rome. The question with which this confronts us is one we all face: Why is it that, even when we are doing what we take to be God's will for us, we oftentimes still have such great difficulty in accomplishing it?[7]

Life requires patient trust in God's infallible timing, even when it seems the clock has stopped. The same God who sent His Son to earth "in the fullness of time" can be trusted with our minutes, days, hours, and years. He uses time to arrange the right circumstances, work in the lives of others, and prepare us for what He has prepared for us.

Just as Londoners adjust their wristwatches to Big Ben, let's align our hearts to God's agenda and say with the psalmist, "My times are in Your hands" (Psalm 31:15).

John Flavel wrote in 1678 that we often see life's events like "the disjointed wheels and scattered pins of a watch." But in due time, he said, we'll see "the whole, united in one frame and working in one orderly motion."[8]

That's something we can depend on—around the clock.

Headwinds

God writes straight with crooked lines.

—A Portuguese Proverb

How often I've been frantic and panicked at a situation that defied instant solution. I could either lose my mind or I could decide to rest on God's promises as He unraveled the knots, untangled the problems, and resolved the issues with His infinite wisdom and in His infallible timing.

The Bible calls this waiting on the Lord.

The psalmist said, "I wait for the Lord, my whole being waits, and in His Word I put my hope" (Psalm 130:5).

Isaiah 30:18 says, "Blessed are all who wait for Him!"

James said, "Be patient, then, brothers and sisters, until the Lord's coming. See how the farmer waits for the land to yield its valuable crop, patiently waiting . . ." (James 5:7).

And Jude said, "Keep yourselves in God's love as you wait for the mercy of our Lord Jesus Christ" (Jude 1:21).

Waiting doesn't mean inaction, of course. If you're waiting for a wife, you might need to ask a woman out for lunch. If you're looking for a job, you'll probably have to fill out applications. We do what's possible while waiting for God to work the problem from His angle. I've always found it wise to knock on a lot of doors without trying to force them, trusting the Lord to open the ones He chooses and to find others I knew nothing about.

Contrary winds swirl around us, directing us to the right places and people at the right time. He turns curses into blessings, and delays into fulfillments. Paul's voyage began to zig and zag in ways that made no sense, but the Lord was controlling the winds.

In 1942, a group of about fifty volunteers from the Army Air Corps signed on to a top-secret and very dangerous mission. Sixteen air crewman trained day and night for clandestine bombing raids that were almost suicidal in nature, all under the command of James Doolittle.

Sergeant Joe Manske was a gunner on Aircraft Number Five. The planes took off from a carrier in the middle of a storm. They flew their mission and were returning home against tremendous headwinds that slowed their progress and depleted their fuel. The crew of Number Five realized that without a miracle they would crash at sea in the darkness of night.

In the back of the Mitchell B-25 bomber, Sergeant Manske sank to his knees and earnestly prayed. As he did so, something strange happened. The winds began to shift direction, and what had been a headwind slowly turned into a tailwind of about twenty-five miles per hour, which began pushing the planes toward their landing sites.

According to Navy meteorologists, that kind of wind never occurred during that time of year. The plane made it to China where all five crew members bailed out and were rescued.[9]

We encounter headwinds in life, but even in the most difficult times we can unbuckle our harnesses, kneel down in the darkness, and pray. When God's children pray in Jesus' name, somehow, in God's timing, the circumstances take a strange turn and end up working for our good; we know not how (see Romans 8:28).

That's the kind of God we have, and you can trust Him!

His wisdom is sublime,
His heart profoundly kind;
God never is before His time,
And never is behind.[10]

—J. J. Lynch

Isn't That Something!

God only can so control the forces of nature and the acts of men that the resulting history shall teach like a parable and shine like a prophecy.

—Thomas Kinnicut Beecher
(in his sermon on Paul's Shipwreck, 1914)

My father once told me that his aged sister, Eva, and her husband, Ernie, decided to see what the ocean looked like. They lived in East Tennessee and neither had ever been to the coast. So they left home in their old car, took the winding roads through the mountains, and finally a day or two later came to Myrtle Beach. They got out, gazed at the endless expanse of shimmering water and its cresting waves, and marveled.

"Well, isn't that something?" said Ernie.

"It sure is," said Eva.

Then they got in their car, turned around, and returned home, their curiosity satisfied!

In Acts 27, Paul, Luke, and Aristarchus wanted to turn

around and go home. They'd had enough of this ocean. Paul was going as one of the prisoners. The other prisoners were likely going to Rome to satisfy the need for human victims in the arena, but Paul was in another class, a celebrated prisoner who possessed Roman citizenship.[11]

Luke was Paul's doctor and biographer; and Aristarchus, a devoted Christian from Thessalonica, had probably made himself Paul's servant or slave so he could tend to the apostle's needs (see Acts 27:1-2).[12]

The three Christians had boarded a local freighter in the harbor of Caesarea, ending Paul's two years of imprisonment there. The ship sailed north to Sidon and docked, where Paul was allowed to visit friends. Putting to sea from there, the vessel sailed along the coast of Asia Minor (modern Turkey), making intermittent stops.

At Myra, the Roman officer found a larger ship headed to Rome, but the voyage was arduous from the beginning. The ship struggled to Crete, where it should have harbored for the winter, as Paul advised. But the captain pressed on, wanting to get his cargo and crew to Rome.

What he got instead was a typhoon like the one that had terrorized Jonah's ship 700 years before. This was no ordinary storm. The Spirit of God was behind the winds and waves. The course of Paul's life was being driven by the circumstances, but the circumstances were being driven by God.

Our Lord's plans for us are synchronized far more precisely than we realize, and He often uses circumstances to guide us. Sometimes the compass is spinning so fast that we can't get our bearings, and life feels out of control. But God is always on His throne.

My friend Reese Kauffman was the owner of a thriving factory in Indianapolis that made, among other things, all the car horns for General Motors. Every GM product produced in America carried a horn built in his plant. Kauffman Industries stockpiled hundreds of thousands of car horns in a 20,000-square-foot warehouse with ceilings twenty-four feet high.

Reese told me, "On our last day at work before Christmas while my workers were celebrating, I got a message from GM that all our horns were defective and could not be used—not one of them. The horror of that message hitting during the Christmas season was terrible. All those beautiful parts we'd been producing for weeks were nothing but worthless scrap. Our whole investment was suddenly a staggering liability. I had to tell my workers that our products were flawed, our inventory worthless, their jobs in jeopardy, and our company in crisis."

Reese said, "I cried out to God for mercy and help. For two long weeks, all of us lived under a cloud. I prayed earnestly and sought to trust the Lord with the burden. Then after the first of the year, the director of purchasing for General Motors came down and listened as I made the case for the accuracy of our work."

To Reese's amazement, the GM representative agreed. "Our investigations show that we sent you the wrong die. It wasn't your fault; it was ours. We sent you a tool from the morgue. All those weeks you put into the design and production of those horns, charge it to us. We'll bear the responsibility and reimburse you for all your expenses."

The ensuing check from GM allowed Reese to buy an adjacent piece of land to expand his plant. What appeared to be a disaster turned into a great blessing, and the wealth it produced allowed Reese to eventually leave his business and devote the next thirty years of his life to leading one of the largest missionary movements on earth—Child Evangelism Fellowship—without ever taking a penny of salary.

That's what our Lord can do.

Isn't that something!

Study Questions

---

1. Read Acts 27:3-8. How is God's perfect timing evident in this passage, even in the midst of all the temporary setbacks it caused the apostle Paul?

2. How do we typically react when we encounter setbacks like Paul faced in Acts 27? How can we change our attitudes to reflect trust in God in the midst of these situations?

3. Read Psalm 130:5. What happens when we wait on the Lord and trust in His Word instead of focusing on our fears and the setbacks we've faced?

4. Focusing on the truth that God can use setbacks for our ultimate good, what shift should occur as we seek a heavenly perspective?

For further individual or group study, check out *The Mediterranean Sea Rules Study Guide* and *The Mediterranean Sea Rules Video Series,* both available at medsearules.com.

Mediterranean Sea Rule #3

Speak Your Mind without Losing Your Leverage

Much time had been lost, and sailing had already become dangerous because by now it was after the Day of Atonement. So Paul warned them, "Men, I can see that our voyage is going to be disastrous and bring great loss to ship and cargo, and to our own lives also." But the centurion, instead of listening to what Paul said, followed the advice of the pilot and of the owner of the ship. Since the harbor was unsuitable to winter in, the majority decided that we should sail on, hoping to reach Phoenix and winter there. This was a harbor in Crete, facing both southwest and northwest.

—Acts 27:9-12

SOFT SKILLS

If only we realized that everything which enters our life is ordered by God, and we acted in accord with this, then should we maintain our composure and conduct ourselves with unruffled serenity.[13]

—ARTHUR W. PINK

When I was a younger man, I worked so hard that I lived in constant fatigue, and I wasn't mature enough to control my anger when provoked. Looking back, I'm ashamed of how I could tear into someone. Saying even the right words in the wrong spirit can inflict a lot of pain on a marriage, a home, a church, or on any other set of relationships. We can be right in our opposition but wrong in our disposition.

Proverbs 12:18 says, "The words of the reckless pierce like swords, but the tongue of the wise brings healing."

Though not completely cured, I've worked on becoming more patient. We need to say the right words with the right spirit and then wait for the Lord to use our input. It takes time for wise counsel to penetrate biased minds.

Good debaters know they seldom change a person's opinion during the debate itself. It's afterward, upon reflection, that minds begin to change.

In Acts 27, the apostle Paul was in an awkward place. He was a prisoner but he had a good relationship with Julius, the centurion guarding him. The seasoned apostle knew from his own experiences on the sea (and perhaps by an impression from the Lord) that sailing was foolhardy as the winter approached. He was an experienced mariner who, as I said, had already been shipwrecked three times. He sensed approaching danger, but the centurion, the captain, and the owner of the ship discounted his warning.

Notice Paul's reaction to his rejected advice. He didn't fly into a rage or lose his composure, to the best of our knowledge, though his own life was at stake. He probably said more than Luke recorded, for this was a serious discussion; but in any case, he spoke his mind without losing his leverage.

We must be diplomatic, not defiant or defensive, in pressing our point.

We're not infallible, but the Word of God is. When accurately interpreted, it speaks much-needed truth to our age. We have tremendous confidence in the validity of a biblical worldview. As a student of the Bible and a preacher of the gospel, I hold deep convictions. So do you. But we have to speak the truth without damaging our cause.

The Bible says, "My dear brothers and sisters, take note of this: Everyone should be quick to listen, show to speak and slow to become angry, because human anger does not produce the righteousness that God desires" (James 1:19-20).

The London-based website The School of Life carried an article titled "How to Be Diplomatic," which said:

> Diplomacy is an art that evolved initially to deal with problems in relationships between countries. The leaders of neighboring states might be touchy on points of personal pride and quickly roused to anger; if they met head on, they might be liable to infuriate each other and start a disastrous war. Instead, they learnt to send emissaries, people who could state things in less inflammatory ways, who wouldn't take issues too personally, who could be more patient and emollient. Diplomacy was a way of avoiding the dangers that come from decisions taken in the heat of the moment. In their own palaces, two kings might be thumping the table and calling their rivals by abusive names; but in the quiet negotiating halls, the diplomat would say, "My master is slightly disconcerted . . ."

The writer went on to say, "We still associate the term 'diplomacy' with embassies, international relations and high politics, but it really refers to a set of skills that matter in many areas of daily life. . . . Diplomacy is the art of advancing an idea or cause without necessarily inflaming passions or unleashing a catastrophe."[14]

That's just what Paul did. He was plain-spoken but not unpleasant, and he advanced his view without rupturing relationships.

Psychologists call this having *soft skills*. *Hard skills* are the technical skills and factual knowledge you need for your job—engineering, mathematics, theology, athletics, or whatever it is. Soft skills have to do with our people skills, our social graces, our communication savvy, our personality traits and self-management and attitudes.

Management consultant Peggy Klaus said that when people look back over their careers, their regrets and frustrations and failures are usually not connected so much with their hard skills but with their soft skills.[15]

All this requires wisdom, maturity, and good temper. Paul had those, and so he didn't ruin his relationships. As a pastor who has dealt with thousands of people for decades, I finally came to a simple conclusion: If someone came to me unhappy about something, they were probably right. If they came to me unhappy about everything, they were probably wrong. Like the Israelites in the desert, they had simply developed a complaining spirit.

Paul counseled but didn't complain. He spoke his mind,

told the truth, trusted God, and waited for others to see, as they finally did, that he was right all along!

Psalm 141:3 has been a useful prayer for me and I'm glad to share it with you: "Set a guard over my mouth, Lord; keep watch over the door of my lips."

When the Majority Is Wrong

Guard your words, mind what you say,
And you will keep yourself out of trouble.

—Proverbs 21:23, The Voice

I considered opening this chapter by telling you the stupidest thing I've ever said, but there were too many options and some are too upsetting to me. But here's an innocuous example. On one occasion, Katrina and I were invited to the home of Joe Rogers, the U.S. Ambassador to France. Did I mention I get flustered in the presence of VIPs? We walked up the steps, and Ambassador Rogers himself opened the door to greet us. I was so nervous, I said, "Mr. Ambassador, my name is Katrina Morgan."

He looked at me quizzically, but without missing a beat he stuck out his hand and said, "Hello, Katrina." I started to introduce Katrina, but what could I say? I was so horrified that I didn't speak another word. I let the real Katrina do the talking.

It's hard to keep from saying stupid things. But it's

equally hard to say the right things in the right way, in the right spirit, and for the right reasons. Paul did so in Acts 27, but the centurion listened to the pilot instead of to the preacher, and "the majority decided that we should sail on" (verse 12).

The majority was—and often is—wrong.

Truth isn't determined by popularity polls, and current trends can be treacherous. Jesus followers march to the beat of a different drummer. That means we may be shunned for speaking truthfully and counted fools for conveying wisdom. That's all right. Just give it time. The truth doesn't change. In Acts 27, Paul simply bided his time and awaited a more favorable moment to be heard.

How many marriages and relationships would be strengthened by patient wisdom! Most of us—including me—suffer a compulsory appetite for giving our opinion. Jesus, on the other hand, sometimes spoke loudest by His silence. I'm thinking of doing a Bible study on "the silences of Jesus."

There's an old phrase sometimes used in the Bible: "He held his peace." It means there's a time for us to *say* our peace and a time to *hold* our peace.

Wisdom is knowing which time it is.

Proverbs 17:27 (CSB) says, "The one who has knowledge restrains his words, and one who keeps a cool head is a man of understanding." The *Good News Translation* puts it: "Those who are sure of themselves do not talk all the time. People who stay calm have real insight."

Paul didn't badger, and soon Julius, the captain, and the owner of the ship had doubts about their own judgment, along with an elevated respect for Paul's. Ecclesiastes 3:7 says that there is a time to speak and a time to remain silent. Harping is for musical instruments.

The apostle's reaction also demonstrated his faith in God's ability to vindicate him. Sometimes we have to leave our case in Christ's hands. When we're aligned with His truth, He will validate us in the future, even if, at the moment, others think we are wrong.

Soon everyone on the ship knew Paul's advice had been best, and he gained a level of influence that allowed everyone on board to be saved. Paul even allowed himself to say, in effect, "I told you so" (see verse 21).

Christian students shouldn't be afraid to state their case in a secular setting; godly employees should share their testimony with unsaved coworkers; Christ followers have an obligation to pass along the gospel with family and friends; and all of us who know Christ should advance biblical positions on moral issues, even if they have political ramifications. But the world around us will notice our demeanor before they listen to our debate. That's why the Bible tells us to speak the truth in love (see Ephesians 4:15).

There's also a caution here.

The multitude is often wrong, and their journey will end in disaster. Jesus spoke of this in Matthew 7:13-14, with many heading down the road to ruin. On the ship, Paul's voice would have prevented exposure to the storm, the loss of the cargo, and the destruction of the ship—if only they had listened.

When someone is warning you about a certain action, listen carefully. My wife—the real Katrina Morgan—seldom hesitated to let me know what she thought. Over time, I learned she was almost always right. It wasn't just women's intuition. It was the wisdom of a godly wife.

We must never be afraid to speak the truth personally or publicly, nor hesitate to share the gospel and advocate a biblical worldview. But few minds are changed by argumentative nagging or relentless talking. It takes time for sensible words to sink into the quicksand of another person's gray matter. So speak the truth and leave it to God to make the impression.

It's better to be right today and thought wrong than, like most people, be wrong today and thought right.

Study Questions

1. Read Acts 27:9-12. How does Paul's disposition remain civil despite his opposition to the plans?

2. Paul's opposition had no immediate effect, but with time the crew came to respect him for having given this warning. How does it change our mindset to know that truth will eventually prevail, even if we are disregarded in the moment?

3. Read Proverbs 12:18. What does this warning about the words of the reckless and the wise have to do with Paul's disposition as he warns the captain against his charted course?

4. What does James 1:19-20 say about our speech, and how can we take that warning to better reflect Christ in the way we express our disagreement?

For further individual or group study, check out *The Mediterranean Sea Rules Study Guide* and *The Mediterranean Sea Rules Video Series,* both available at medsearules.com.

Mediterranean Sea Rule #4

Let Divine Grace Hold You Together

When a gentle south wind began to blow, they saw their opportunity; so they weighed anchor and sailed along the shore of Crete. Before very long, a wind of hurricane force, called the Northeaster, swept down from the island. The ship was caught by the storm and could not head into the wind; so we gave way to it and were driven along. As we passed to the lee of a small island called Cauda, we were hardly able to make the lifeboat secure, so the men hoisted it aboard. Then they passed ropes under the ship itself to hold it together. Because they were afraid they would run aground on the sandbars of Syrtis, they lowered the sea anchor and let the ship be driven along.

—Acts 27:13-17

THE PERFECT STORM

. . . they used helps, undergirding the ship . . .

—ACTS 27:17, KJV

Verse 14 is dramatic: "Before very long, a wind of hurricane force, called the Northeaster, swept down." The Greek word Luke used for "hurricane force" is *typhonikos,* or typhonic. The words "typhoon" and "hurricane" describe exactly the same weather event. By this time, the captain was attempting to navigate the southern coast of Crete, but the storm blew the ship into the open Mediterranean and far from any viable landfall.

Verse 15 says, "The ship was caught by the storm," and here the Greek verb means "to be seized with great violence." The same term was used in Luke 8:29 of a demon violently seizing a man.

An ancient granary ship caught in a storm of this intensity was a floating coffin. Try to imagine it! Monster winds. Mountainous waves. Biting rain. Howling wind. A small ship plunging downward, rising upward, timbers cracking, masts crashing, passengers heaving, timbers leaking.

"She's breaking apart," screamed one of the old salts as wood splintered. The captain ordered the strongest sailors to lower the frapping ropes, which would encircle the ship and, hopefully, keep it from falling to pieces. The *New King James Version* says, ". . . they used cables to undergird the ship." The *Amplified Bible* says, ". . . they used support lines [for frapping] to undergird and brace the ship's hull."

In his classic 1880 book, *The Voyage and Shipwreck of St. Paul,* James Smith wrote of a British naval officer named Henry Smartley who had seen this done to a Russian ship in 1815. Smith also described an 1837 voyage during which Captain George Back was forced to do the same.[16]

Admiral William Henry Smyth, in his 1867 book on nautical terms, defined the word "frapping" as "The act of passing four or five turns of a large cable-laid rope around a ship's hull when it is apprehended that she is not strong enough to resist the violence of the sea. This expedient is only made use of for very old ships, which their owners venture to send to sea as long as possible."[17]

This brings me to the single-most thrilling lesson the Lord has taught me from Acts 27, which involves another Greek term used by Luke in the original account.

The word for "ropes" in Acts 27:17 is *boetheia* (pronounced bo-a-tha'-a): "Then they passed ropes under the ship itself to hold it together."

This isn't the common Greek word for "ropes." *Boetheia*

literally means "helps," as we see it translated in the old *King James Version*. As in English, this basic term can be either a verb or a noun. He will *help* you (verb). *Help* is coming (noun).

This word *boetheia* occurs only two times in the New Testament: here and in Hebrews 4:16, which says, "Let us then approach God's throne of grace with confidence, so that we may receive mercy and find grace *to help* us in our time of need" (italics mine).

Take a moment to think through the cross-reference! Just as the sailors encompassed the hull of their ship with ropes to keep it from falling apart, so too God wraps the cords of His grace around us to keep us from doing the same.

How wonderful!

The Lord permits storms, but He doesn't want us falling apart, which, left to ourselves, we would do. So the Lord invites us to come in prayer to His throne and obtain the needed cables of grace and mercy that will compose and strengthen us.

We are undergirded by grace, held together in the storm by the cables of God's care, which we access at the throne of grace.

That's the meaning of this strange word "undergird." I read about a woman who couldn't understand why her husband always ended his prayers by saying, "Now, Lord, undergird us this day with Your strength." She never asked him what "undergird' meant, but she would always suppress a giggle. After his death she mentioned it to someone. "It was so strange," she said. "It always reminded me of some kind of garment worn under the clothes."

Well, now you know!

Undergirding is the idea of being wrapped in the ropes of God's strengthening grace. Do you need grace to help you now in a time of need? Do you need undergirding steadiness? You'll find it at the throne of grace.

Here's a prayer you can make your own. It was first offered during World War II on the floor of the United States Congress by Senate Chaplain Dr. Frederick Brown Harris:

> Eternal Father,
>
> Strengthen us, we beseech Thee, in the inner man, by the renewing, sustaining, undergirding grace which is able to keep us from falling and failing. So may our hearts be steadied and stilled, purged of self, emptied of strain and stress, filled with peace and poise, satisfied with each new morning just to wake up and find Thee there. For Thine is the kingdom to which the future belongs, and the power, and the glory, forever and ever.
>
> Amen.[18]

Learning the Ropes

No matter where God's children find themselves—in a cell or in a sanctuary—each of us can boldly approach the throne of grace to discover a Father who loves us and gives us His undivided attention.

—Petr Jasek

According to Ecclesiastes 4:12, a three-strand cable is hard to break. I've been on the verge of falling apart many times—from fear, anxiety, anger, exhaustion, or overwhelming tasks or situations. God's means of grace have been the cords that have held me together—especially the strands of Scripture, hymns, and prayers.

I'm not alone. In his book, *Imprisoned with ISIS,* Petr Jasek recounted his arrest and imprisonment by Sudan's Islamist regime in 2015. Petr was in Sudan representing Voice of the Martyrs to aid persecuted Christians. He was seized, tried, falsely convicted as a spy, sentenced to life behind bars, and imprisoned with ISIS warriors, who horribly beat and abused him in the crowded cell. In all, Petr spent 445 days in Sudanese prisons.

He wrote, "I felt trapped in the claustrophobic cell, surrounded constantly by incessant Muslim prayers and Arabic recitations of the Koran. . . . I worried constantly about my family, about how they would be able to make ends meet. I even struggled to formulate my own prayers. If I wasn't careful, I knew I could lose my mind."

The ISIS warriors beat him until his whole body was bruised with welts and wounds. They also made him stand and turn toward the toilet whenever they recited their prayers.

> *Allahu Akbar* became a near-constant sound in the prison cell. It's part of the Muslim call to prayers, and each man repeated it incessantly over the course of the day, one hundred times each time they prayed. Confined to this tiny room, I watched my cellmates bow and listen to words from the Koran. In the midst of all the murmuring voices and repetitious prayers, I started to worry about my mental health.
>
> In the final days of January, as my Muslim cellmates were praying, the Lord began to give me songs. Watching the Muslims bow their faces to the ground triggered the memory of a hymn that my father taught me when I was a little child: "Every Knee Shall Bow." During our underground church discipleship meetings

> in Czechoslovakia, we sang the hymn spontaneously and often, and in my prison cell, those same words began to rush into my mind. . . . Five times each day, as I stood near the bathroom of the cell to face the toilet, I remembered the refrain, "Every knee will bow, every tongue confess that You're the Lord."
>
> By reminding myself that one day, every person's knees would bow before my Lord, I began to internalize the eternal reality of my victory in Christ, and my sanity stayed intact.
>
> In moments when I was most worried about my mental health, the Holy Spirit reminded me of Philippians 4:7: "And the peace of God, which surpasses all understanding, will guard your hearts and your minds in Christ Jesus."[19]

Later, Petr was given a Bible and a hymnbook, and as the Sudanese authorities moved him from prison to prison, he found remarkable opportunities for leading prisoners to Christ. And though he was separated from his family and friends, a chorus of prayer was rising daily to the throne of grace, and there Petr found mercy and grace to help in time of need. He learned afresh that one doesn't have to be in a palace or even in a church to approach the greatest throne in the universe. Prayer, Scripture, and the hymns we've known from childhood are God-designed for prison cells, lonely apartments, hospital rooms, business suites, basketball courts, or wherever you encounter your next moment of vulnerability.

Keep the three-stranded cable of Scripture, hymnody, and prayer close at hand. They stretch from heaven to earth, and from God's throne room into the center of your heart.

When you get to the end of your earthly rope,
Let God undergird you with His heavenly hope.

STUDY QUESTIONS

1. Read Acts 27:13-17. How many references to the storm's strength and the ship's weakness does this short passage have?

2. How does the study of the word for "rope" help us understand the mercy and grace of God that strengthens us as we seek Him?

3. Read Ecclesiastes 4:12. What does this description bring to mind when read after Acts 27?

4. Read Philippians 4:7. How can this verse change our hope when our situation stays the same?

For further individual or group study, check out *The Mediterranean Sea Rules Study Guide* and *The Mediterranean Sea Rules Video Series,* both available at medsearules.com.

Mediterranean Sea Rule #5

Jettison Hindering Cargo

We took such a violent battering from the storm that the next day they began to throw the cargo overboard. On the third day, they threw the ship's tackle overboard with their own hands. When neither sun nor stars appeared for many days and the storm continued raging, we finally gave up all hope of being saved.

—Acts 27:18-20

Lighten the Ship!

Let us put everything out of our lives that keeps us from doing what we should. Let us keep running in the race that God has planned for us.

—Hebrews 12:1, NLV

It's strange how a crisis can rearrange our priorities. When Katrina and I were new parents, we faced a calamity. In the wee hours one morning, our baby started crying in her small nursery. Katrina slipped out of the bedroom, then started screaming. Flames were leaping through the living room. I tried to snuff them out while Katrina snatched Victoria from the crib. The air was heavy with smoke, and I used my fist to break a window. The incoming air fanned the flames and we had to flee. I was wearing only a robe and shorts.

Padding through the wet grass to the neighbor's house, we opened the door and walked in. People seldom locked their doors in that rural neighborhood. Bessie came down the steps having just arose, saw us, and froze. In shock, I stupidly said, "Bessie, I'm not wearing any pants. Do you have any I can borrow?"

In all her life, Bessie had never expected her young pastor to say such a thing, but when she saw the flames through the window it made sense, and she scrambled to call the volunteer fire department and get us blankets and clothing. Katrina and I lost almost everything, but it didn't really matter to us—because we had saved the baby!

(Later, that baby, now grown, claimed she's the one who saved us!)

Perhaps you'll agree: Only a few things really matter, especially in view of time and eternity.

In 1 Corinthians 7:31, the Lord tells us that time is short and the days are urgent, so those of us who accumulate possessions should use them without becoming absorbed with them or attached to them, "for the world in its present form is passing away."

The 276 souls aboard Paul's ship were no longer concerned with the precious cargo they had stowed below deck. Luke wrote, "And because we were exceedingly tempest-tossed, the next day they lightened the ship" (verse 18, NKJV).

Verse 19 says, "We threw the ship's tackle overboard with our own hands." And verse 38 adds, ". . . they lightened the ship and threw out the wheat into the sea."

In this ship, the hull would have been filled with grain,

which also served to ballast the vessel. On top of the grain would be cargo, and atop the cargo would have been the ship's tackle. We have no idea of the total value, but it didn't matter. Life itself was at stake.

Adam Gellert, a motivational speaker and entrepreneur, wrote:

> Recently, God gave me a vision that has changed my perspective on what it really means to cast our cares on Him. He showed me the image of having to throw the cargo overboard on a ship during a storm. And it made me wonder, why did people do that during Bible times? We see in the story of both Jonah and Paul that they were on a boat that was in danger of sinking because of a storm. The crew starts throwing its cargo overboard, so why did they do this?
>
> To lighten the ship. A heavy cargo makes a ship sit deeper in the water, which is dangerous in shallow water. The crew threw the cargo overboard so the ship would sit higher in the water in case they were blown near land, where their boat would get destroyed on the shallow reefs, rocks, and harbors. If the bottom of the ship ran aground miles from any shore, they faced the prospect of being tossed into the sea. Thus, when you are faced with life or death, everything (even the food) becomes expendable. . . .

> With this analogy, God was showing me that there were some things I was holding onto, that I needed to throw away to lighten my ship. The storms that will hit all of us at some point or another, can serve as a way to force us to throw away some things we view as "precious cargo," such as a job, money, pride, rebellion, or anything else that keeps us from relying solely on Him. When the seas are quiet and the ship of life is cruising along smoothly, we aren't challenged to let go of some things that could make us stronger in the long run.
>
> What cargo do you need to throw overboard to lighten the load?[20]

As I read this, my mind went to everything I've recently read about decluttering. Many interior designers and life coaches have advocated ridding our lives of the endless miscellany that litters our surroundings. One expert suggests going through the house, handling every item you own, and asking yourself if it sparks joy. If not, toss it.[21]

The things that most hinder my joy are nonmaterial. It's attitudes like anxiety, anger, frustration, bitterness, regret—and sinful habits that creep into my life like rats on a ship. We can't literally throw those things in the garbage can, but with the help of crucial Bible verses we can nail them to the cross and let the Lord have them.

Colossians 3:8 says, "But now you must also rid

yourselves of all such things as these: anger, rage, malice, slander, and filthy language from your lips."

James 1:21 says, "Therefore, get rid of all moral filth and the evil that is so prevalent and humbly accept the word planted in you, which can save you."

Anything that hinders us from staying afloat or threatens a successful voyage is disposable. Live simply, and when you run into a storm, ask God what you need to toss overboard.

Lighten the ship and you'll brighten your life.

Below Deck

Storms can cause me to discard what I used to value.

—Rick Warren

What's going on below deck with you?

Seafaring in the first century and in the nineteenth weren't all that different, so we can learn a lot about Paul's voyage by thumbing through old shipping books. One of the most useful textbooks for sailors of yesteryear was *Ainsley's Examiner in Seamanship*. Here's a section of the curriculum:

Q: What is meant by jettison?
A: To throw overboard cargo or equipment to lighten or relieve the ship when in danger.

Q: Under what circumstances is such an act warranted?
A: When it is done in a storm to lighten the ship, or after getting aground, for the purpose of getting the ship off, its object being the preservation of the vessel and crew.

Q: Suppose your ship has sprung a leak, your pumps do not keep it under, and other attempts fail, what would you do?
A: Lighten the ship by throwing some of the cargo overboard.

Q: What part of the cargo would you throw overboard first?
A: When possible that part of the cargo which is of least value and greatest weight should be chosen, but such considerations should not be allowed to cause any delay where the danger is imminent.[22]

It's amazing my ship doesn't sink in the harbor, because I clutter it with so many unneeded and unhelpful actions, attitudes, baggage, and tackling. James told us to get rid of anything evil and to humbly accept the word planted in us (see James 1:21).

Here is a sample manifest of hindering cargo, along with some verses that may encourage you. I've left blank spaces at the end because of the myriad of other crates we cram below deck.

- **Possessions**. These are the things that clutter our houses or apartments. Don't be overly sentimental with them (except maybe heirlooms to pass to the next generation). Simplify your home and regularly take boxfuls of clutter to the trash or to a charity. Beware of buying everything you want, which is sometimes a besetting sin for me. See 1 Timothy 6:6-18.

- **Money**. Establish the habit of tithing—giving 10 percent of your income to the Lord—and go beyond that. Something about this habit keeps us mentally healthy about our finances. See Proverbs 3:9-10.

- **Habits.** Sinful patterns and addictions, like pornography, drug or alcohol abuse, immorality in your relationships, or cursing, can weigh down the soul. Confess these as disgusting sins before Almighty God, accept them as self-destructive, determine to turn from them, and seek counseling therapies to break the habits. Never give up. Keep fighting with every weapon at your disposal. See Galatians 5:16-25.

- **Anxiety**. Study Psalm 37, Matthew 6, and Philippians 4. Those are the Bible's three most definitive passages about worry. Also see Psalm 55:22 and 1 Peter 5:7.

- **Bitterness**. Learn to give your hurts and those who inflicted them to God; He can settle accounts better than you can. And free yourself from brooding over the past. See Isaiah 43:18-19.

- ______________________________

- ______________________________

- ______________________________

There's an endless amount of cargo to be tossed overboard so we can travel lightly and rightly. We're headed toward a heavenly harbor, toward a city that shimmers with light, toward an eternity only Jesus could provide and an inheritance only we can enjoy. He warned against "the worries of this life and the deceitfulness of wealth" that can "choke the word, making it unfruitful" in our lives (Matthew 13:22).

Is anything hindering your voyage? Slowing your progress? Weighing you down?

Jettison it!

Get rid of anything that displeases our Lord, and set both your mind and heart on things above (see Colossians 3:1-4).

We gain by losing, and we thrive with pruning. It's time

for you to make progress, even if some of your hopes, habits, possessions, or plans end up in Davy Jones's locker.

How often less is more!

STUDY QUESTIONS

---

1. Read Acts 27:18-20. What does this passage say about the moment of hopelessness they had in this trying time? How does the fact that even the apostle Paul faltered and lost hope comfort us in the midst of our hopelessness?

2. What do all of the listed verses and their focus on heaven teach us about the potential distractions of material possessions and earthly worries? How can we overcome these through the grace of God?

3. Read Colossians 3:8 and James 1:21. How do these verses help explain the spiritual application of Acts 27?

4. Choose one of the categories listed that may be hindering your relationship with God, and spend some time reading the corresponding passages and praying about them. What action steps have the scriptures shown you moving forward in these areas?

For further individual or group study, check out *The Mediterranean Sea Rules Study Guide* and *The Mediterranean Sea Rules Video Series,* both available at medsearules.com.

Mediterranean Sea Rule #6

Expect God to Do Exactly as He Has Said

After they had gone a long time without food, Paul stood up before them and said: "Men, you should have taken my advice not to sail from Crete; then you would have spared yourselves this damage and loss. But now I urge you to keep up your courage, because not one of you will be lost; only the ship will be destroyed. Last night an angel of the God to whom I belong and whom I serve stood beside me and said, 'Do not be afraid, Paul. You must stand trial before Caesar; and God has graciously given you the lives of all who sail with you.'

So keep up your courage, men, for I have faith in God that it will happen just as he told me. Nevertheless, we must run aground on some island."

—Acts 27:21-26

SEA CHANGE

Though neither sun nor stars were seen, Paul knew the Lord was near; And faith preserved his soul serene when others shook with fear.

—JOHN NEWTON

"We finally gave up all hope of being saved," Luke wrote in verse 20—and the "we" seems to have included Paul. He wasn't a superhero. As we study the book of Acts and the Pauline epistles, we sometimes see him struggling, anxious, fighting discouragement. Not even the great apostle could withstand the endless battering of a prolonged tempest.

But while Paul was tossing in terror on the high seas, Jesus of Nazareth was watching from the throne of grace in heaven, just as years before on a mountainside He had kept an eye on His disciples who were struggling on the wind-tossed Sea of Galilee (see Mark 6:47-48).

Now at the Father's right hand, our Lord occupies a place of ultimate power, and His eye sees everything that happens to us.

On this occasion, Jesus summoned an angel to His side and said something like this: "You'd better rush down there and intercept that ship with a message to Paul. He's on the verge of despair."

The celestial being plunged from heaven's balustrade, dove through the atmospheres like a HALO jumper, landed precisely on the boat, and materialized in Paul's dark little corner of the tossing vessel. How long the angel ministered to Paul, we don't know. The apostle only repeated two short sentences of the conversation: *Do not be afraid, Paul. You must stand trial before Caesar; and God has graciously given you the lives of all who sail with you.*

This word from the Lord caused a sea change in the heart of the apostle Paul. Without waiting for morning, he gathered the crew, gave them the message from heaven, and said, "So take courage, men, because I believe God that it will be just the way it was told to me" (verse 25 CSB).

Notice the phrase "take courage."

Courage is mental toughness. It's the determination to remain strong of spirit when you feel mightily like collapsing in weakness. It's a frame of mind that's willing to persevere and withstand discouragement and danger because of known truth from an unseen source. True courage only comes from fixing our thoughts on the person of Jesus Christ, who rose from the dead and now reigns in heaven.

Older translations use the word "cheer" instead of

"courage." The Greek word has a range of meanings: to dare, to be bold, to be of good courage, to be cheerful, to be confident.

Do those words describe you right now?

Notice that they are commands, imperatives, orders from the Commander, and non-optional attitudes for God's children. Our Christ-infused courage allows us to remain cheerful at heart. It's an internal gyroscope, spinning around at the center of our lives and keeping us balanced and steady, courageous and confident.

Billy Graham once preached before the British Royal Family in the chapel of Windsor Castle. His text was Acts 27:25, and he said,

> [Paul] was on a ship when a storm arose. The ship was being tossed about by the wind and waves. The men were frightened. Paul went to his room and prayed. When he came out, his face glowed with a look of peace and assurance as he made this statement: "Be of good cheer, I believe God."
>
> There are many storms in the world today. There are storms of atheism, materialism, and internationalism. Homes are broken. Juvenile delinquency is rampant. Crimes are on the increase. There are other storms in the personal life of people—storms of discouragements,

bereavements, confusions, frustrations. But Paul said to be of good cheer.[23]

Whether we're a monarch on the throne or a beggar on the street, we must take courage and be of good cheer because Christ has spoken into our situation, using sixty-six infallible books to relay His message. We will never exhaust His truth. We have a surer word than angels can give and a deeper word than the world knows. We have the Word of God.

It will always be even as He has said.

As I write these words, I'm reviewing my attitudes, trying to make sure my life radiates with Jesus-given courage, cheer, confidence, and conviction, based on His worth and His Word. It isn't in my nature but in His super-nature, which He shares with all who are "in Christ."

Paul's words and demeanor lifted the other sailors and passengers, buoying them up with fresh hope. The One who holds the waters of the sea in the hollow of His hand will keep us strong in the storms and confident in the crises.

And He will use us to impart courage and cheer to others in the tempest.

As God Has Said

When you are in the dark, listen, and God will give you a very precious message for someone else when you get in the light.

—Oswald Chambers

Recently, I took my grandson Owen to the San Diego Zoo. When we returned to our car, it was dented. Another guest had bumped it and left a note on the windshield. I went back to the hotel discouraged, and I had to preach that evening.

Lying on the bed, I closed my eyes. Suddenly I heard Owen reading aloud. He was reading the scripture for the day from his *Daily Light*, and the last verse said, "In this world you will have tribulation, but be of good cheer, for I have overcome the world."

I can't tell you how my heart leapt at hearing a nine-year-old voice reading 2,000-year-old words telling me to be of good cheer.

This is what Paul told the mariners: "Be of good cheer. God has promised to save us all, and I believe it will be just as He said!" Jesus had sent His angel to shore up Paul's courage in the darkness, and now he had a message for others in the light. He believed it would happen even as the Lord had told him.

That's one of the Bible's classic definitions of faith: it will be to us even as the Lord told us. Everything changes in a crisis when God speaks, when the Lord gives us a verse of Scripture.

How wonderfully does the Word of the Lord come to us! The Lord knows when and how to speak to us, and He does so primarily through His Word. He comes to us in our weakness, in our sorrow, in our fear.

The renowned nineteenth-century evangelist Dwight L. Moody was crossing the Atlantic in November 1892 when his ship suffered an accident at sea and drifted out of the normal sea lanes. Water poured into the lower cabins, and the sailors began preparing the lifeboats, though there were too few for the passengers. In the rough seas, the crippled vessel lurched and pitched and appeared to be sinking. Even the fearless Moody was terrified.

"That was an awful night," he wrote, "the darkest of all our lives—several hundred men, women, and children waiting for the doom that seemed to be settling upon us. No one dared to sleep. . . . We were all together in the saloon of the first cabin. . . . The agony and suspense were too great for words. . . . It was the darkest hour of my life."

The drama continued into the next day, then the next. But in the terror of the moment, God gave Moody Psalm 91, which he read to the passengers, one hand holding his Bible as the other arm gripped a post for support.

"It was a new Psalm to me from that hour," Moody later said. "The eleventh verse touched me very deeply. It was like a voice of divine assurance, and it seemed a very real thing as I read: *He shall give His angels charge over thee, to keep thee in all thy ways.*"

Moody went on to say, "God heard my cry and enabled me to say from the depth of my soul, *Thy will be done.* Sweet peace came to my heart. . . . Out of the depths I cried upon my Lord, and He heard me and delivered me from all my fears."

Two nights after the initial accident, Moody was awakened by his son, telling him that another ship had seen the distress flares and had come to help. All the passengers were saved.[24]

The Lord often speaks to us loudest in the storms because we need to know that His voice is far more powerful than the roaring waves and howling winds. Verses we might otherwise pass over suddenly become precious. Chapters of Scripture we've often read before catch fire in our hearts. Even a random phrase of the Bible—like "be of good cheer"—affects us so deeply that we never afterward forget it.

God doesn't waste storms. They will pass, but the assurances God gives us in their midst will stay with us for the rest of our lives. In the process, the Lord will give us a precious message for other tempest-tossed souls.

So take courage! Be of good cheer!

It will be just as He has said!

Reading the Refrigerator

There is a wonderful sense of being in God's presence as you let your mind dwell on His words.

—T. W. Wilson

I took some of my older grandchildren to visit my friend Sally Wilson Pereira, whose father, T. W. Wilson, had been Billy Graham's oldest and closest associate. I wanted the youngsters to hear original stories about Billy and Ruth Graham as I recorded a podcast with Sally.

When we entered her kitchen, I was astonished by all the magnets on her refrigerator. They covered every square inch, from bottom to top, front and sides. When I looked more closely, I saw they were all various Bible verses.

Sally saw us studying the magnets, and she explained, "Whenever I'm too discouraged to even open my Bible, I stand here and read my refrigerator."

I love it! The Bible is an armory of little swords, each one lethal to the devil. Find ways to surround yourself with God's Word and you cannot remain discouraged. There's a wonderful sense of being in God's presence as you let your mind dwell on His words, especially in storms.

He gives courage and cheer, and we know it will be even as He has said.

Study Questions

1. Read Acts 27:21-26. What hope do these verses bring to the passengers and sailors coming on the heels of the utter hopelessness described in the previous passage?

2. What glimpse of the perfect timing of God is given in this passage as the angel brings hope in their least expecting moment?

3. Read Mark 6:47-48. How does this passage give us a greater insight into the heart of Christ looking into the desperate situation of His disciples and coming down to help them?

4. Read Psalm 91:11. What does the promise of this verse mean for us when we navigate the storms of life?

For further individual or group study, check out *The Mediterranean Sea Rules Study Guide* and *The Mediterranean Sea Rules Video Series,* both available at medsearules.com.

Mediterranean Sea Rule #7

Minister in the Moment

Just before dawn Paul urged them all to eat. "For the last fourteen days," he said, "you have been in constant suspense and have gone without food—you haven't eaten anything. Now I urge you to take some food. You need it to survive. Not one of you will lose a single hair from his head." After he said this, he took some bread and gave thanks to God in front of them all. Then he broke it and began to eat. They were all encouraged and ate some food themselves.

—Acts 27:33-36

Ships in the Night

Buried with Christ and raised with Him too,
What is there left for me to do?
Simply to cease from struggles and strife
Simply to walk in newness of life.

—The favorite hymn of Rev. John Harper

Now that Paul had regained his nerves, he was ready to minister in the moment. Undoubtedly, he privately reassured and prayed with his brothers, Luke and Aristarchus. He encouraged the crew to take some nourishment and spoke to them of God's care and concern. He gave the young centurion, Julius, grounds for hope. In the middle of the storm, he led the crew in a prayer of thanksgiving and urged them to eat. His cheerfulness surely affected the others as he ministered in the moment, serving, in effect, as the ship's chaplain.

Paul had never filled out a chaplain's job application. He hadn't expected to be part of the chaplaincy corps. But in that moment he had a mission, and he ministered.

Sometimes we're able to plan our work in advance—preparing a Bible lesson, putting committee meetings into our calendar, or arranging to go on a missions trip. But most of the ministry God gives us occurs in the moment, especially in those moments when people need a ray of cheer.

Just as I was writing this paragraph, a young man knocked on my door and we spent the next hour talking about preaching, pastoring, and the priorities of a church service—all subjects that had been on his mind. His name wasn't on my calendar that day, but he was on God's schedule for me, and I took the interruption as from the Lord.

There are other occasions when one has to *become* the interruption and inject Jesus into the picture. Two weeks ago, I took a taxi to pick up my truck at the auto dealership. The driver had a Bible tucked into the pocket of the back seat, and I asked, "Do you read this Bible?"

"No," he said. "It belonged to my aunt and I keep it there to feel close to her."

"Well," I said, "it's good to have a Bible, but it's better to read it. I read mine every day. Let me tell you about its message." Over the next fifteen minutes I shared the story of Jesus with him, and by the end of the ride he prayed to receive Christ as Savior. That hadn't been on my agenda for the day, but, praise God, it was on His!

Sometimes our most momentous work is done in unexpected minutes, and sometimes even in unwelcome hours.

John Harper was a Scottish boy who came to Christ and started preaching when he was a teenager. Later he became the pastor of Paisley Road Baptist Church in Glasgow, and the congregation grew from twenty-five members to over five hundred. In 1912, he was invited to Chicago to preach at Moody Memorial Church. He was thirty, a widower, and the father of a six-year-old daughter named Nina, who traveled with him.

They boarded their ship with some excitement, for it was the maiden voyage of the *Titanic*. Three nights later when the great ship struck the iceberg, John took Nina to the deck and handed her to a White Star employee with instructions to get her into a lifeboat.

Meanwhile John ministered in the moment, helping people to safety while sharing the gospel with everyone he could. He gave up his life vest and his place on a lifeboat.

Shortly afterward, as he thrashed around in the icy waters, a man clinging to flotsam drifted toward him, and John cried to him, "Are you saved?"

"No!"

Harper shouted the words of Acts 16:31: "Believe in the Lord Jesus, and you will be saved."

The man drifted into the darkness, but minutes later the current again swept him close to John, who shouted, "Are you saved?"

"No!"

"Believe in the Lord Jesus, and you will be saved!"

With that, Harper lost his grip and slipped to his grave, but the other man was rescued. He later described himself as "John Harper's last convert."[25]

I don't know why God spared Paul yet took John Harper, but I do know that the biggest concern for both men was ministering in the moment—doing what they could for Christ as one second merged into the next.[26]

When you learn to minister in the moment, you'll never be out of a job. Nor bored. Nor plagued with a sense of uselessness.

And by the way, little Nina (Annie Jessie Harper) survived the shipwreck and was raised by her godly uncle. She worked at a Bible college and became a devoted pastor's wife who, throughout her life, also devoted herself to ministering in the moment. She became the longest surviving Scottish *Titanic* survivor.

Nina and her husband had two children, including a daughter, Mary, who grew up, married, and had children of her own.

Mary later said, "My eldest son, when he was about ten, was doing a project at school about the *Titanic*, and I told him about it. When I said, 'Your grandmother was on the *Titanic*,' he asked me, 'Did she drown?' I explained that no, she hadn't, or else we wouldn't be here!"[27]

Sometimes we miss the obvious. If we are here—anywhere—the Lord has need of us. On the deck of a sinking ship or in the back seat of a taxi or in a million-dollar mansion, the Lord has work for us in the moment. He has placed us where we are for such a time as this. When you put this book down and go on with your day, look around for what He wants you to do in the strength of His Spirit. Little things done with divine power yield great results.

On the land or sea, at home or abroad, minister in the moment, and do it for the Master! You are His chaplain to a seasick, storm-tossed world.

Saving the Day

How much can Jesus Christ do through you? Anything and everything. God is limited only by the measure of our availability to all that He makes available to us.

—Major Ian Thomas

My great-grandson, Clay, is three years old and fully potty trained, but the other evening he had an "accident" at a restaurant, and he was embarrassed and very upset. My daughter, Victoria, scooped him up and took him out to the car. "Don't worry about it," she said. "I happen to have a change of clothes right here in this bag." She got him cleaned up and changed, and as they were going back into the restaurant, he looked up at her and said, "Minnie, you 'sav-ed' the day for me."

Victoria started crying. "That's what mothers do all the time," she said. "We save the day for people, but we seldom get such a sweet acknowledgment."

The Lord Jesus found us when we were messed up, and He saved the day for us. Now He wants us to do the same for others, even as Paul saved the day for his terrified companions.

When Katrina and I were pastoring, we prepared ourselves before going to church each Sunday by reminding ourselves of MBWA—*Minister By Walking Around.* We borrowed the idea from the then-popular business acronym MBWA—*Manage By Walking Around.* After Katrina's disability kept her from walking, she would still come to church in her battery-powered wheelchair and zoom around talking to people. She brought a lot of joy as she rode around with her joystick, though parishioners sometimes had to jump out of her way. She learned to *Minister By Zipping Around*, and I can still see her radiant smile.

There's a sense in which the whole of personal Christian service is simply that—ministering by walking or running or zipping around, knowing that the full resources of Christ are available to those who are fully available to Him.

We don't always get sweet acknowledgments, but you never know when you'll save the day for someone as you minister in the moment.

HARDTACK

After he said this, he took some bread and gave thanks in front of them all. Then he broke it and began to eat.

—ACTS 27:35

When is the best time for gratitude? Maybe now! Perhaps when you're cold, shivering, sodden, seasick, and at the end of your earthly resources. That's how the sailors and passengers felt in Acts 27, as Paul took some hardtack and gave thanks to God in front of them all (see verse 35).

It's the Living Bible that calls it "hardtack," but I suppose that's accurate. Imagine a piece of bread, purchased near the harbor in Crete several weeks before. It must have been as dry as a brick (unless the seawater had gotten to it). Yet Paul was thankful for it, and he knew his spirit of thanksgiving would affect the others and encourage them to partake of rations God had provided.

It's when we're most likely to feel sorry for ourselves that we should shift the focus as quickly as possible to thanksgiving and to praising the Lord.

Praise not only magnifies the Lord; it elevates the heart and alleviates the hurt.

When we feel our emotions heading on a downward track, we should strive to set our minds on an upward trajectory. Instead of saying, "This is so terrible," we must say, "Even in this bad situation, let's find some things for which to thank God."

The quality of gratitude has become an academic sensation, with psychologists learning that it has the power to literally change the presets of our personalities. There's a heavenly algorithm to it. It's a way of calculating grace. Counting your blessings lets you multiply joy, subtract sorrow, and gain the dividends of a balanced mind. It changes the factors of life, alters the equations, and rounds up the heart. It's a formula for faithfulness and an independent variable you can employ with every problem. Gratitude helps us figure that misfortune is only a fraction of life and that our blessings reach to the vanishing point.

That about sums it up.

The darker the night, the farther a candle in the window casts its welcoming glow. In the same way, some of God's sweetest blessings appear in the darkest times, as evidence He is still near, still dear, and still working, and that nothing has changed about Jesus' promise of an abundant life (see John 10:10).

We may not always be thankful *for* the storm, but we can be thankful *in* the storm. Our pilot, the Lord Jesus Christ, is here to save the day. So we might as well thank the Lord and pass the hardtack.

Study Questions

1. Read Acts 27:33-36. The people on board the ship drew great hope from Paul's words. Can you think of a time in your life when someone's words brought a surge of hope or relief to you?

2. How is Paul able to minister in the moment despite his dire circumstances, and how can we learn from this to be more ready to minister by walking around?

3. What are some ways you have seen God take a moment of chaos and use it for ministering in the moment, and how do they connect to this account of Paul?

4. Read John 10:10. How does Jesus' promise seem to conflict with the situations we find ourselves in? What can we do to focus on the promise of Jesus rather than the plight of our circumstances?

For further individual or group study, check out *The Mediterranean Sea Rules Study Guide* and *The Mediterranean Sea Rules Video Series,* both available at medsearules.com.

Mediterranean Sea Rule #8

Don't Underestimate the One Percent

Altogether there were 276 of us on board. When they had eaten as much as they wanted, they lightened the ship by throwing the grain into the sea. When daylight came, they did not recognize the land, but they saw a bay with a sandy beach, where they decided to run the ship aground if they could. Cutting loose the anchors, they left them in the sea and at the same time untied the ropes that held the rudders. Then they hoisted the foresail to the wind and made for the beach. But the ship struck a sandbar and ran aground. The bow stuck fast and would not move, and the stern was broken to pieces by the pounding of the surf. The soldiers planned to kill the prisoners to prevent any of them from swimming away and escaping. But the centurion wanted to spare Paul's life and kept them from carrying out their plan. He ordered those who could swim to jump overboard first and get to land. The rest were to get there on planks or on other pieces of the ship. In this way everyone reached land safely.

—Acts 27:37-44

Unsinkable Saints

I looked for someone among them who would build up the wall and stand in the gap before me on behalf of the land so that I would not have to destroy it, but I found no one.

—Ezekiel 22:30

Luke was a precise historian, and his details add depth to his writing. In verse 37, he tells us there were 276 souls aboard the sinking cargo ship. Among them were three followers of Christ—Paul, Luke, and Aristarchus.

Three among 276—in rough, round figures, that's one percent.

The Lord had mercy on the entire ship because of the one percent.

It reminds me of the story of Sodom in Genesis. It was an exceedingly evil city, dominated by sensual and sinful practices. We don't know the population of the city, but let's say it was 1,000. Abraham said, in effect, "Lord, would you spare the city for the sake of ten righteous people?" And the Lord replied in the affirmative. Unfortunately there weren't ten such people to be found, so the angels quickly ushered out the handful of godly folk and rained fire and brimstone on the rest.

If only there had been ten—which perhaps would have been one percent.

In Judges 7, Gideon had an army of 32,000 men, but the Lord pared them down to just 300—about one percent—and gave them the victory.

Earlier we learned that the majority is often wrong. The lesson here is the opposite—the minority is often strong, stronger than we realize when Jesus is among us. Jonathan Blanchard, the founder of my alma mater, Wheaton College, said, "The minorities have done the good in this world; the majorities only register it."[28]

The followers of Jesus are usually a minority in any community, nation, school, team, business, factory, or military unit. They're often marginalized and ignored, often disdained. But they—you and I—are spiritually magnetic, drawing the world toward Christ in ways we don't even realize.

This is why Paul told Christian spouses to stay, if possible, with their non-believing marriage partners, for "an unbelieving husband is consecrated by that union—touched by the grace of God through his believing wife," and vice versa (1 Corinthians 7:14, The Voice). This doesn't mean our loved ones are automatically saved and justified because of our faith, but they are blessed and affected in ways beyond their understanding.

Jesus compared this strange effect to leaven, saying, "The kingdom of heaven is like yeast that a woman took and mixed into about sixty pounds of flour until it worked all through the dough" (Matthew 13:33).

Guess what percentage of yeast is typically used in bread? According to a typical baker's percentages, the flour is listed as 100 percent, the salt content is 2 percent, and the yeast is 1 percent.

When my wife, Katrina, became disabled, I was the chief cook and baker in the house. I'm not a baking expert—far from it. But I know what it is to mix flour, warm water, a bit of salt, and a packet of yeast into a ball of dough and watch it rise. The yeast is a living microorganism that eats away at the sugars in the flour and produces gas (carbon dioxide) that fills the dough like a balloon.

One percent!

Jesus was vitally concerned about the one percent. Remember His story about the shepherd who had a hundred sheep, but one was missing? Leaving the ninety-nine in the fold, he went out into the night searching and finding the lost one—the lost one percent (see Luke 15:4).

A small minority of Christians changes the chemistry of any environment, so don't worry if you're among the few. There were only 120 Jesus followers in Jerusalem, but when the Holy Spirit came upon them, they turned the world upside down.

The Lord often places us in situations where we're outnumbered but not outdone. He chooses the weak things of the world to confound the strong (see 1 Corinthians 1:27).

When Frances Ridley Havergal was a teenager, her widowed father moved to Germany seeking medical treatment, and Frances found herself the only Christian out of 110 girls in a school in Dusseldorf. She was literally the one percent. She later said, "It was very bracing. I felt I must try to work worthy of my calling, for Christ's sake. It was a sort of nailing my colors to the mast."[29]

When Jill Briscoe became a Christian, she was the only one in her family and she felt very much alone. But a friend encouraged her by saying, "Don't say, 'I'm the only one.' Start saying, 'I'm the first one.'"[30]

In 1788, there were 80 students at Hampden Sydney College and a handful of faculty members—about 100 people altogether on the campus, and almost all hostile to Christianity. One percent of them—a single student named Cary Allen—came to Christ, and his presence sparked a riot on campus. But it also sparked a revival that spread through the school to other colleges and helped kindle the Second Great Awakening in America.[31]

A small minority of godly people, committed to Jesus Christ and to the authority of Scripture, can forestall judgment and siphon grace into a society or group in a way that far exceeds their proportional presence.

Little is much when God is in it; and Jesus plus one is always the majority.

That's why the 276 souls on Paul's ship were saved. He, Luke, and Aristarchus were unsinkable, and through them grace was extended to the rest.

It's hard to submerge people who are filled with the Spirit, anchored to the Rock, latched to the buoys of the Bible, and held up by the everlasting arms. Their power far exceeds their percentages.

"Was You Not Afraid?"

The waves of the sea were mighty, and raged horribly. The ship not only rocked to and fro with utmost violence, but shook and jarred . . . No one could . . . keep one's hold on anything. . . . Every ten minutes came a shock against the stern or side of the ship, which one would think should dash the planks in pieces.[32]

—John Wesley

A terrible storm churned up the Atlantic on Sunday, January 25, 1736, trapping a small vessel, the *Simmonds*, on which a handful of German Moravian Christians were trying to hold a worship service—on the deck! Right in the middle of their hymn, a tremendous wave hit the ship, broke over the hull, split the main sail in pieces, and poured water down through the decks. Everyone screamed in terror, except for the Moravians, who missed hardly a note of their hymn.

One of the most terrified passengers was a young aspiring missionary who was not even truly a converted Christian. The calmness of the Germans amazed him, and he afterward approached one of them and asked, "Was you not afraid?"

"I thank God, no," came the reply.

"But were not your women and children afraid?"

"No, our women and children are not afraid to die."

Young John Wesley was astonished at the difference of attitude between the Christians and the others on board, including himself. Later, back in England, he attended a Moravian worship service, discovered for himself the heart-warming love of Jesus, and went on to lead one of the greatest revivals in Christian history—the Wesleyan Revival.[33]

Christ followers are a small group of people standing on the deck of a storm-tossed world, singing praises to God because of the hope within us. Our ability to praise God in the storm—indeed to sing psalms and hymns and spiritual songs!—and to remain calm in the tempest is one of the greatest testimonies we ever bear.

We never know who is watching, but we always know God is working.

For the Good of Others

Although the ship in which he sailed,
By dreadful storms was tossed;
The promise over all prevailed,
And not a life was lost.

—John Newton

Dr. A. W. Tozer wrote, "A real Christian is an odd number anyway. He feels supreme love for One whom he has never seen, talks familiarly every day to Someone he cannot see, expects to go to heaven on the virtue of Another, empties himself in order to be full, admits he is wrong so he can be declared right, goes down in order to get up, is strongest when he is weakest, richest when he is poorest, and happiest when he feels worst. He dies so he can live, forsakes in order to have, gives away so he can keep, sees the invisible, hears the inaudible, and knows that which passes knowledge."

We *are* an odd number—we're the one percent, and sometimes more! The followers of Christ are a paradox to the world. We present the minority report to the world. But I believe with all my heart that God uses us in invisible ways to forestall judgment and advance grace to this globe.

Marie Monsen, a missionary in China, happened to be in a certain city when panic erupted. A notorious army of outlaws was rumored to be headed that way. Marie was in the town leading a women's Bible conference, and the women were seized with fear at the news, knowing the reputation of this rogue army. Marie prayed with them, and the Lord gave them a verse, Genesis 18:32 (KJV): "I will not destroy it for the ten's sake." The women said, "We have more than ten here!"

Marie later wrote:

> We lay down in our clothes that night. There was some shooting and some heavy bombing too at first, then all was silent. Early in the morning we were told that the bandits had left the city in great haste. They were said to have heard that a large army was coming to relieve the city and was not far off. We were a very happy group of women that day. We had personally experienced the presence of God, for one of His own promises had been literally fulfilled before our eyes.[34]

Marie felt that the presence of a small group of believers had spared the entire city.

Spurgeon preached, "Paul was put into a ship—into a ship among thieves and other criminals—into a ship among sailors and soldiers, who were none of the best in those days, but he was put there for their good. This, then, I would lay down as a general theory—there are multitudes of Christians who are in places very uncomfortable, and, perhaps, very unsuitable for them, who are put there for the good of others."[35]

If you're overwhelmed by the godlessness around you in your work, school, or environment, remember that the Lord has put you there for the good of others. It's my belief the only thing standing between our world and the judgment of God is the presence of Christ-devoted believers on this planet. The mysterious presence of God's Spirit in you casts an effect within the radius of your personality.

Peter said, "Live such good lives among the pagans that, though they accuse you of doing wrong, they may see your good deeds and glorify God on the day He visits us" (1 Peter 2:12).

Don't be intimidated, discouraged, or bullied.

Just be Jesus in your world—as Paul was on the ship.

And so it was that the vessel was pulled by the winds and tides toward the coast of Malta. Hoping to run the ship aground, the sailors cut the four anchors, raised the foresail, and let the ship drift toward shore. But the ship struck a sandbar, which caught the bow like a vise. The stern began breaking apart in the surf, and everyone leaped overboard as the ship disintegrated. Some swam to shore while others clung to pieces of the wreckage, but when a tally was made, everyone was accounted for. They were shivering but safe.

But Paul's troubles weren't over.

Study Questions

1. Read Acts 27:37-44. How is the mercy of God evident in the soldiers' decision not to kill the prisoners?

2. What role do you think Paul's presence among, and interaction with, the Roman guard had in the decision to spare the prisoners? What can we learn from that about being a light for God and reflecting Christ in all our interactions?

3. Read Matthew 13:33 and Luke 15:4. What do these passages show about the care God has for the one percent?

4. Read 1 Peter 2:12. What does this verse say about the importance of living a life for God that causes others to see Him in you?

For further individual or group study, check out *The Mediterranean Sea Rules Study Guide* and *The Mediterranean Sea Rules Video Series,* both available at medsearules.com.

Mediterranean Sea Rule #9

Shake the Serpents into the Fire

Once safely on shore, we found out that the island was called Malta. The islanders showed us unusual kindness. They built a fire and welcomed us all because it was raining and cold. Paul gathered a pile of brushwood and, as he put it on the fire, a viper, driven out by the heat, fastened itself on his hand. When the islanders saw the snake hanging from his hand, they said to each other, "This man must be a murderer; for though he escaped from the sea, the goddess Justice has not allowed him to live." But Paul shook the snake off into the fire and suffered no ill effects. The people expected him to swell up or suddenly fall dead; but after waiting a long time and seeing nothing unusual happen to him, they changed their minds and said he was a god.

—Acts 28:1-6

Our Ancient Foe

We are shipwrecked on God and stranded on omnipotence.

—Vance Havner

Only once in my hiking have I confronted a rattlesnake, and he gave me plenty of advance warning by his clattering. That was over fifty years ago but the evil glint in his eye has made me nervous ever since. Recently, while hiking in the Southwest, I was told to watch for rattlesnakes and copperheads, and that made me paranoid. I constantly scanned the pathway ahead of me. A time or two, I thought I saw a snake and jumped back about two feet. But in each case it was just a curved stick of wood.

Paul wasn't so fortunate. He pulled himself onto the Maltese beach feeling like a drowned rat, then staggered to his feet to scan the situation. All around him, another 275 souls were doing the same, but in the darkness and bitter rain it was hard to gather one's wits.

Suddenly, with torches and loud voices, the nearby population appeared. They weren't hostile. On the contrary, the islanders "showed us unusual kindness" (the Greek word is *philanthropia*, from which we get our word "philanthropy"), racing to find garb and grub. They built a huge bonfire to warm the shivering seamen. Always the servant, Paul ventured into the bushes to find some loose firewood. (Elisabeth Elliot wrote, "In times of deepest suffering it is the faithful carrying out of ordinary duties that brings the greatest consolation.")

As he placed the wood on the fire, a viper, driven out by the heat, struck at him and fastened its fangs into his hand. It wouldn't let go, and everyone saw the coiling, writhing snake clinging to Paul's hand with its vise-like jaws.

The islanders expected Paul to begin swelling, collapse in spasms of pain, and die in agony. Paul's concierge doctor, Luke, could only look on in helpless horror.

With a mighty exertion of strength, Paul shook off the creature and flung it into the fire, where it perished. As for the apostle, he suffered no ill effects, except, perhaps, a bit of bleeding on his hand, which Luke could handle.

This is literal history, but it's hard to avoid the obvious analogy.

The Bible compares Satan to a serpent from Genesis 3, when he tempted Adam and Eve until we come to Revelation 20, when that old serpent, the devil, will be flung into the "lake of burning sulfur."

His venom is deadly, but there is an antidote—the blood transfusion of Calvary. Jesus took the fangs of Satan on the cross, and our Lord's blood is our immunization.

Like Paul's viper, Satan can scare us, alarm us, attack us, wound us, and cause us pain. He tries to hang on to us. But because of the life-giving serum of Jesus' blood and righteousness, he cannot harm God's children in any ultimate way. And in the power of our Lord Jesus Christ, we can fling that serpent into the fire.

Don't be surprised at the spiritual warfare you'll face as you go through life. The devil may send snakes to bite you, enemies to hound you, problems to dog you, and fears to torment you. If the storm doesn't work, he'll send a shipwreck; if that doesn't work, he'll send a snake.

But we are more than conquerors through Jesus Christ our Lord! Through our Lord Jesus Christ, we have the victory, and this is the victory that has overcome the world, even our faith (see Romans 8:37; 1 Corinthians 15:57; 1 John 5:4). Satan has no answer for the death of Christ and no defense against our Lord's resurrection. None of his weapons will vanquish the blood of Christ, and none of his schemes will prevail over the Christ of the blood.

In the Bible, there are several titles for our ancient foe—Satan, the devil, the serpent. But the title that the New Testament writers often used was the "evil one."

If Satan's snake eyes are trained on you, take these verses to heart.

- *And lead us not into temptation, but deliver us from the* ***evil one*** (Matthew 6:13).

- *My prayer is not that you take them out of the world but that you protect them from the* ***evil one*** (John 17:15).

- *In addition to all this, take up the shield of faith, with which you can extinguish all the flaming arrows of the* ***evil one*** (Ephesians 6:16).

- *I write to you, young men, because you are strong, and the word of God lives in you, and you have overcome the* ***evil one*** (1 John 2:14).

- *We know that we are children of God, and that the whole world is under the control of the* ***evil one*** (1 John 5:19).

- *The One who was born of God [Jesus Christ] keeps them safe, and the* ***evil one*** *cannot harm them* (1 John 5:18).

- *But the Lord is faithful, and He will strengthen you and protect you from the* ***evil one*** (2 Thessalonians 3:3).

Let's sum up: Ask God to protect you from the evil one—you and your loved ones. That's a biblically authorized prayer. Trust God when you're under attack, keeping the shield of faith firmly gripped. Remember that in Christ, despite how you may feel, you are strong, His Word lives within you, and you are an overcomer. The whole world is under the devil's control—all except for God's children, and Jesus keeps us safe from Him. He cannot ultimately harm us, because Christ, in His faithfulness, has won the victory and granted us His peace, presence, and protection.

The prince of darkness grim,
We tremble not for him.
His rage we can endure
For, lo, his doom is sure.

—MARTIN LUTHER

Dangling Snakes

Too many people allow their situation to get the best of them. A lot of people let their circumstances get them down. You must be able to shake things off. It is important to shake it off and keep going. Don't look back but look forward.

—Tommy Ray Banks, Sr.

Right now, imagine a snake is fastened to your hand. Practice shaking it off into the fire. Give your hand a good fling. That's what we must learn to do with things. It's a metaphor that works and a motion I have to practice often.

I sometimes call it the Hyatt Rule. My coach in high school was John Hyatt, and he occasionally drove me home from after school events. For years, I'd chewed my fingernails, and it was a habit I couldn't shake. In the car, he looked over and asked me why I was chewing my nails to the quick, and I told him it was a habit.

"Well, I can tell you how to break it," he said. "Every time you notice your fingers in your mouth, take them out." That was the whole of his advice, but it worked! After a week or two, the habit was broken for good.

It's also a transferable habit. Whenever you find yourself complaining, stop doing it and say, "Praise the Lord!" Whenever you find yourself feeling blue, stop and ask God for a restored soul. In other words, learn to shake off the clinging vipers. When problems come to my mind, I recite a memorized scripture and shake them off.

Here are things I have to shake off, and the verses that have helped me.

REGRETS

From unkind words to my teachers, to misunderstandings with my parents, to moments of failure as a caregiver, I have regrets in life. But Genesis 45:5 has been a powerful word for me. Joseph, speaking to the brothers who, years before, had sold him into slavery, said, "Don't be upset or angry with yourselves any longer because of what you did. You see God sent me here ahead of you to preserve life" (The Voice). It's time for you to stop beating yourself up. Shake it off, for God can even use our worst moments for His purposes.

LOSS

In the past five years I've lost my wife, Katrina, who passed away from complications of multiple sclerosis. I've faced numerous moments when God's plans differed from my own. Each of these has produced many nights of bad dreams, and I've felt the losses deeply. But the Lord gave me Isaiah 43:18-19, and whenever I feel down, I quote these wonderful words: "Forget the former things; do not dwell on the past. See, I am doing a new thing! Now it springs up; do you not perceive it? I am making a way in the wilderness and streams in the desert."[36] (This became especially meaningful later the same year when I visited En Gedi, where David fled from King Saul. There I saw literal streams gushing from the mountain rocks of the Negev desert.)

HURTS

How easy to brood over slights and snubs from others! I'm an expert brooder, and my feelings of hurt can produce anger, bitterness, and even vindictiveness. We have to shake off this cycle of reactions, and the only way is by focusing on the cross. From the time, years ago, when I suffered at the hands of a hit-and-run driver, my go-to verses have been Romans 12:18-19: "If it is possible, as far as it depends on you, live at peace with everyone. Do not take revenge, my dear friends, but leave room for God's wrath."

CRITICISM

My shake-it-off verse in the face of criticism and all manner of other things is Philippians 1:18: "But what does it matter?" The apostle Paul was being disparaged and misused by some of the Christian leaders in Rome. But he shook it off and said, "What does it matter?" He was putting into practice Proverbs 12:16: "Fools show their annoyance at once, but the prudent overlook an insult."

DISCOURAGEMENT

To succeed in life, we have to learn to shake off discouragement. Since the beginning of my ministry, I've leaned on 1 Corinthians 15:58: "Therefore, my dear brothers and sisters, stand firm. Let nothing move you. Always give yourselves fully to the work of the Lord, because you know that your labor in the Lord is not in vain."

GRUDGES

My dad, as good as he was, knew how to carry a grudge, and so I learned from the best. Ephesians 4:26 (TLB) says, "If you are angry, don't sin by nursing your grudge. Don't let the sun go down with you still angry—get over it quickly." In other words, shake it off!

GUILT

When it comes to guilt, I embrace the biblical word "abundant." The Bible says He *abundantly* pardons us from all our sins (see Isaiah 55:7 NKJV). It talks about "God's *abundant* provision of grace and of the gift of righteousness" that enables us to reign in life through one Christ Jesus (Romans 5:17). Psalm 31:19 says the Lord stores up an *abundance* of good things for us. And Psalm 145:7 tells us to celebrate God's *abundant* goodness. He is able to bless us *abundantly* "so that in all things at all times, having all that you need, you will abound in every good work" (2 Corinthians 9:8)—all because Jesus came to give us life and give it more *abundantly* (see John 10:10 NKJV). Focusing on that puts guilt in its place—under the blood of Jesus.

I have these words both highlighted and underlined in red in my old, tattered copy of Martyn Lloyd-Jones's book *Spiritual Depression:* "You and I must never look at our past lives; we must never look at any sin in our past life in any way except that which leads to praise God and to magnify His grace in Christ Jesus."[37]

Now, I know some things are not easy to shake off. Some require counseling, sessions of godly therapy, time to mature, and the resources of all the means of grace God has provided. Addictions, abuse, trauma—this life isn't easy. Between the storms, the shipwrecks, and the snakes, we overcome only by God's amazing grace. But this I know full well: God does not want you going through life with serpents dangling from your hands.

Remember Acts 28:5: "But Paul shook the snake off into the fire and suffered no ill effects."

You can do the same!

Study Questions

---

1. Read Acts 28:1-6. What is the connection here between the physical serpent that bites Paul and the idea of spiritual warfare that believers face as they work for the Lord?

2. How does Paul's resilience in the face of this attack show the courage he has as a follower of Christ? How can we take hold of this courage as we work for the Lord and fight off attacks from the devil?

3. Read Romans 8:37, 1 Corinthians 15:57, and 1 John 5:4. What do these verses say about the conquering power of our faith in Christ Jesus? How can we live victoriously in light of this powerful gift from God?

4. Read Isaiah 55:7, Romans 5:17, and 2 Corinthians 9:8. How do these verses describe the abundance of God's grace, and how can we take hold of this when we feel the weight of our guilt?

For further individual or group study, check out *The Mediterranean Sea Rules Study Guide* and *The Mediterranean Sea Rules Video Series*, both available at medsearules.com.

Mediterranean Sea Rule #10

Look Around for What Christ Wants You to Do Next

There was an estate nearby that belonged to Publius, the chief official of the island. He welcomed us to his home and showed us generous hospitality for three days. His father was sick in bed, suffering from fever and dysentery. Paul went in to see him and, after prayer, placed his hands on him and healed him. When this had happened, the rest of the sick on the island came and were cured. They honored us in many ways;

and when we were ready to sail, they furnished us with the supplies we needed.

—Acts 28:7-10

There's Always Something to Do Next

Life is too short and eternity is too long and souls are too precious and the Gospel is too wonderful for us to take it easy.[38]

—Vance Havner

The Lord always turns things in a good-ward and God-ward direction for those who love Him, and Paul's snake-bite was no exception. His survival astonished the islanders, and he was immediately taken to the estate of the governor, a man named Publius, who gave Paul, Luke, Aristarchus, and presumably Julius, the centurion, and a few others three days of rest and recuperation. Paul learned that the father of his host was very ill, suffering fever and dysentery. The apostle healed him, and his healing ministry extended to others on the island.

For three months, Paul preached Christ at this isolated outpost. It had never been on his itinerary, but it was on the agenda of God, who was so concerned for the population of Malta that He sent a storm to blow in the world's foremost evangelist.

Imagine how many new believers came from all this, likely including Centurion Julius, slaves condemned to die in the arena, salty sailors, fellow passengers, and native Maltese.

Whatever the circumstances, the apostle Paul was always looking around for what God wanted him to do next. He wasn't finished until the Lord was ready to take him to heaven.

At the end of three months, when the seas were again safe, Julius arranged transport to Italy; and finally—after years of waiting—Paul arrived in Rome, where he rested another three days and then went to work.

The last time we see him in the book of Acts, he is living under house arrest in his own rented dwelling, welcoming all who come to see him, proclaiming the kingdom of God, and teaching about the Lord Jesus Christ—"with all boldness and without hindrance" (Acts 28:31)!

Paul never stopped. Whatever the circumstances, he simply looked around for what the Lord wanted him to do next. Christ never stops using people like that. I can't imagine living without Christ and the work He assigns. We never outgrow it, and even in heaven His servants will serve Him (see Revelation 22:3). There's joy in serving Jesus. And there's happiness in following the Lord of the cross, wherever He goes.

In 1973, a group of Presbyterian churches pulled

away from their liberal denomination and founded the Presbyterian Church in America. They started without a dime, but someone gave $90,000 for world missions to support the only two missionaries they had, who were in Acapulco.

One of those was a man named Dick Dye, and he had been trying to start a church. It was difficult, and he grew discouraged.

"Whenever he got discouraged," said a friend, "he looked up at a cross he could see on a nearby mountain. That encouraged him. Finally, he drove up the mountain to find out about that cross. And when he did, he found it attached to a big hotel."

Dye asked the secretary at the hotel, "Can I speak to the man who runs this establishment?"

"Do you have an appointment?" she asked.

"No appointment. I just want to tell him something."

"What do you want to tell him?" the secretary pressed.

"I want to thank him," Dye responded. The secretary got the owner, and Dye told him, "I'm a missionary from the United States here in Acapulco. I've been discouraged. But I see that cross and it encourages me. I want to thank you for having it up there."

The hotel owner looked at Dye, put his head down on his desk, and began to weep. He wept and wept. Finally, he raised his head and said, "That cross has been up there for years. All I've heard is criticism. You're the first man who ever said thank you. Now, who are you and what do you need?"

"I'm just a missionary," Dye answered.

"Where do you meet?" the owner asked.

"We don't meet anywhere. I don't have any place to meet," Dye said.

"Come with me," the hotel owner instructed. He took Dye to a beautiful chapel and said, "We have church here at 9:00 a.m. and 11:00 a.m. From now on, it is yours at 10:00 a.m. You begin service next week."

That was the beginning of PCA missions. Within a few years, there were four strong congregations.[39]

We can't do much in our own energy, with our own personalities, utilizing our own gifts. But when the Christ of the cross directs our way, there's always something to do next, and the Lord is in the details. Just as Christ fulfilled His Father's will in the power of the Holy Spirit, so too we fulfill His will in the same Spirit's power. We let Jesus of Nazareth live His life, do His work, and speak His words through us.

If you've weathered the storm or recovered from the snakebite, just take a moment now to say, "Thank You, God! Now, what's next? What venture now? What adventure next?"

His grace is sufficient, His purposes are right, His power is sovereign, His truth endures to all generations, and there's no end to His exploits for His people. Believers never come to the end of their future. There is literally no end to it. That's why it's called *everlasting* and *eternal.*

You never know what's next, but He most certainly does! And if you know Him, that's enough!

The Invisible Thread

Life is filled with predictably unpredictable events. There's a special joy given to "What's next, Lord?" teachable saints.

—Lloyd John Ogilvie

After three months on Malta, Julius found an Alexandrian ship with majestic carvings on its bow, and, bidding their new island friends goodbye, the 276 survivors resumed their journey. Paul and his companions finally landed in Italy, and so the apostle made it to Rome, where he rented a house while awaiting his trial before Nero.

There, Paul ministered for two years under the watchful eyes of Roman soldiers, who became a sort of captive audience for his message. It's funny how God turns the tables. The book of Acts ends at that point, but we believe that during this time Paul wrote his famous prison epistles—Ephesians, Philippians, Colossians, and Philemon. Then, according to ancient reports, he was released and traveled with freedom before his final arrest, imprisonment, and execution, which was preceded by his final epistle—2 Timothy.

From the moment of his conversion on the Damascus Road to his death in Rome, Paul had followed the invisible thread.

Once, long ago in a faraway land, there was a young man who always knew the best route to any location, and because of that he was in great demand. He led travelers to distant cities. He guided pilgrims to desired shrines. He led generals and their armies on military campaigns. He led the king and his caravan on diplomatic missions. And always, as he escorted his clients, he held his right hand in front of him as if running it along an invisible thread.

The pathway he chose was often harder than that of other guides, but it always ended up being better. His paths had detours and bypasses, but they always proved the best. His invisible thread never failed to steer him in a way that, in retrospect, was best. Sometimes he himself felt perplexed by the way he was going, but he never doubted the thread of guidance he felt in his right hand.

Few people in this world have ever reached out and felt that unseen thread, but it is there for every one of us. It is the perfect will of God. For every one of us, there is an invisible thread to guide us through our lives. God has an individual plan for each person who is committed to Jesus Christ as Lord and Savior.

Burleigh Law, a missionary aviator in Africa, discovered this in dramatic fashion. One day during his normal flight runs in Congo, he ran into a deadly storm that seemed to sweep toward him from nowhere. It was like Paul's storm.

In the cockpit of his little missionary plane, he lost his bearings as thunderclouds surrounded him on every side. Here and there openings appeared in the clouds, and Burleigh kept turning his plane toward those openings, following little patches of blue like a needle through fabric. Finally, he saw a little landing strip beneath him, and he landed with a sigh of relief.

Suddenly a vehicle came racing up to his plane. A nurse ran to him, saying, "I don't know where you came from, but I know you are an answer to our prayers." A missionary couple had been isolated on this remote mission station. The roads were impassable and the bridges were out. The wife had become seriously ill with a high fever. Early that morning, the Christians in the village had gathered for earnest prayer for help. They had specifically asked God to somehow send help and intervene in the crisis. In response, God arranged patches of blue to guide Burleigh through the storm clouds like an invisible thread, directing his little plane to the ordained spot of earth.[40]

The invisible thread of God's guidance will take you through seas and storms and serpents. He will lead you by land, air, or sea. The power of His cross will preserve and protect you, and the hand that lit the stars will navigate your way.

Give Jesus Christ your life completely, trust Him with the storms, never stop serving Him, and learn to ceaselessly pray:

Jesus, Savior, pilot me
Over life's tempestuous sea;
Unknown waves before me roll,
Hiding rock and treacherous shoal.
Chart and compass come from Thee.
Jesus, Savior, pilot me.

STUDY QUESTIONS

1. Read Acts 28:7-10. This passage show's Paul's willingness to complete the task set before him and then move on to the next work God has for him. How can we better submit our lives in service to God like this?

2. What does the closure in this passage teach us about the way in which God allows us to see our work through and then move on to the next thing He has for us? What is an opportunity God gave you or someone you know to see their work finished and move on to their next service for the Lord?

3. After thinking about the "invisible thread of God's guidance" at work in your life, what is an area where you can submit to God's guidance and trust His plan for you?

4. How will you prayerfully consider the call to "Look Around for What Christ Wants You to Do Next," and how will you prepare yourself to be ready when God calls you into the next step of obedience?

For further individual or group study, check out *The Mediterranean Sea Rules Study Guide* and *The Mediterranean Sea Rules Video Series,* both available at medsearules.com.

Appendix

Psalm 107:23-32

23 Some went out on the sea in ships;
they were merchants on the mighty waters.
24 They saw the works of the Lord,
his wonderful deeds in the deep.
25 For he spoke and stirred up a tempest
that lifted high the waves.
26 They mounted up to the heavens and went down to the depths; in their peril their courage melted away.
27 They reeled and staggered like drunkards;
they were at their wits' end.
28 Then they cried out to the Lord in their trouble,
and he brought them out of their distress.
29 He stilled the storm to a whisper;
the waves of the sea were hushed.
30 They were glad when it grew calm,
and he guided them to their desired haven.
31 Let them give thanks to the Lord for his unfailing love and his wonderful deeds for mankind.
32 Let them exalt him in the assembly of the people
and praise him in the council of the elders.

NOTES

1. See, for example, Michael. S. Heiser, *The Unseen Realm* (Bellingham, WA: 2015), 302-306.

2. http://www.tynebuiltships.co.uk/C-Ships/cityoflahore1911.html.

3.Marguerite McQuilkin, *Always in Triumph* (Columbia, SC: Columbia Bible College, 1956), 84.

4. Ibid., 91.

5. Thomas Goodwin, *An Exposition on the First Chapter of the Epistle to the Ephesians,* in *The Words of Thomas Goodwin,* ed. Thomas Smith (1861-1866; reprinted, Grand Rapids: Reformation Heritage Books, 2006), 1:211.

6. "Young Man Overcomes Illness by Learning Skills from a Near-Dead Art: Watchmaking," by Judy Cole, January 13, 2020, at https://www.goodnewsnetwork.org/reuben-schoots-canberra-australia-makes-a-watch-from-scratch/.

7. Ray C. Stedman in his sermon "God and Shipwrecks," preached April 4, 1971, at https://www.raystedman.org/new-testament/acts/god-and-shipwrecks.

8. John Flavel, *The Whole Works of the Rev. Mr. John Flavel: Volume IV* (London: W. Baynes & Sons, 1820), 348.

9. Barry Loudermilk, *And Then They Prayed* (Barry Loudermilk, 2011), 33-47.

10. Quoted by V. Raymond Edman, *The Disciples of Life* (Minneapolis: World Wide Publications, 1948), 78.

11. William Ramsey, *St. Paul the Traveler and the Roman Citizen* (Grand Rapids: Baker, 1982 reprint edition), 314.

12. Ibid., 316.

13. Arthur W. Pink, *Exposition of the Gospel of John: Three Volumes Complete and Unabridged in One* (Grand Rapids: Zondervan, 1975), Volume 2, page 24.

14. "How to Be Diplomatic" at https://www.theschooloflife.com/thebookoflife/how-to-be-diplomatic/.

15. Peggy Klaus, *The Hard Truth About Soft Skill* (New York: HarperCollins, 2007), 1.

16. James Smith, *The Voyage and Shipwreck of St. Paul* (London: Spottswood and Co., 1880), 108-109.

17. Admiral W. H. Smyth, *The Sailor's Word Book* (London: Blackie and Son, 1867), 321.

18. *The Congressional Record*: Senate, Wednesday, April 7, 1943.

19. Petr Jasek, *Imprisoned with ISIS* (Washington, DC: Salem Books, 2020), 69-70.

20. http://www.activationmovement.com/2017/05/

21. Marie Kondo, *Spark Joy: An Illustrated Guide to the Japanese Art of Tidying* (New York: Ten Speed Press, 2016), preface.

22. Thomas L. Ainsley, *The Examiner in Seamanship* (Cardiff: Thomas L. Ainsley, nd), 180.

23. https://www.chattanoogan.com/2022/10/7/457200/Chattanooga-s-George-Burnham-Was-There.aspx

24. William R. Moody, *The Life of D.L. Moody by His Son* (Murfreesboro, TN: Sword of the Lord Publishers, nd), 4090-407.

25. Moody Adams, *The Titanic's Last Hero* (West Columbia, SC: The Olive Press, 1997), 25.

26. Ibid., 107.

27. https://www.dailyrecord.co.uk/news/local-news/cambuslang-womans-mother-titanic-survivor-2553758

28. Clyde S. Kilby, *Minority of One* (Grand Rapids: Eerdmans, 1959), 6.

29. Charles Bullock, *The Sisters* (London: Home Words Publishing Office, nd), 25.

30. Jill Briscoe, *Here I Am, Lord, Send Somebody Else* (Nashville: Thomas Nelson, 2004), 118.

31. Earle E. Cairns, *An Endless Line of Splendor* (Wipf and Stock Publishers, 2015), 98.

32. John Wesley, *The Works of the Rev. John Wesley, Volume 1* (New York: J & J Harper, 1827), 126.

33. Adapted from Wesley, *The Works of the Rev. John Wesley, Volume 1*, 127.

34. Marie Monsen, *A Present Help* (Shoals, IN: 2011), 21-22.

35. Charles Spurgeon from his sermon "The Church the World's Hope," preached in 1863 and published September 7, 1905.

36. The word "desert" is from other translations.

37. D. Martyn Lloyd-Jones, *Spiritual Depression: Its Causes and Cure* (Grand Rapids: Eerdmans, 1965), 75.

38. Vance Havner, *It Is Time* (Fleming H. Revell Company, 1943), 45.

39. Adapted from "The Power of Thank You" by Beecher Hunter at https://bh.lccatmc.com/pdfs/The-Power-of-Thank-You.pdf.

40. Virginia Law, *Appointment Congo* (Chicago: Rand McNally & Co., 1966), 20-21.